OVERVIEW

"What bad manners you have! Don't eat with your fingers, use your chopsticks!" For many a child in China, Korea, Japan, and Vietnam, this parent's reprimand is one of the first lessons in social manners. For each of these ethnic groups, putting food in your mouth with your fingers is viewed as an ill-mannered, rather animal-like act.

One of my Indian friends, however, has told me, "When I eat with a fork or chopsticks, I lose the pleasure of having a meal. If we eat with our fingers, we can also enjoy the heat of the food, the consistency of the curry, and the texture of what we are eating. For us Indians, our fingers are like a second tongue." We need to move away from the slanted view that eating with the fingers is unsanitary and barbaric, while using eating utensils is the "civilized" way to eat a meal. The culinary arts of the world's various peoples are a cultural heritage developed over the centuries. The best way to ensure full enjoyment of each ethnic group's foods is to eat them in the same manner as they do. Even eating with fingers has a set of manners all its own.

In Asia, the custom of eating food directly with the fingers is found in the Middle East, India, and throughout Southeast Asia with the exception of Vietnam. In all such localities, the hands are normally washed thoroughly before and after the meal. Certainly your own hand which you have carefully washed yourself is a more reliable sanitary tool for eating than the fork or chopsticks washed-

-perhaps haphazardly--by someone else. Moslems, Hindus, and the members of other sects may use only their right hand for eating, with the left hand, deemed less clean, used for other purposes, never coming into contact with food. In localities where eating with the hand is the tradition, people do not use tables or chairs, instead gathering around the food placed on a mat or similar floor covering and using the hands to partake of food from a common central bowl or plate.

In contrast, cultures which use chopsticks apportion the food among those joining in the meal, with each person eating from the individual dishes in front of him. In particular, soup and the staple food, rice, of such "chopstick regions" are served separately to each individual, and small individual bowls have developed in such regions for this purpose.

The three main Western eating utensils, knife, fork, and spoon, first began to appear together on European tables in the 17th century. Chopsticks, on the other hand, have a much longer history and were widespread in China as long ago as the second century B.C. Korea, Japan, and Vietnam, all of which were strongly influenced by Chinese civilization, also came to use chopsticks. Similarly, the peoples of Mongolia and Tibet, both of which border China, are familiar with chopsticks but normally do not use them in their everyday meals.

STAPLE FOODS

In the western areas of Asia, the representative food can be seen as bread, whereas in the eastern regions of the continent, rice would occupy this position. This is true to the extent that in Japanese, the term "eating rice" is synonymous with "having a meal." Let's look for a moment at these staple foods and the methods of preparing them.

First, speaking broadly, in western India and farther west, wheat is an important foodstuff, and it is all ground to flour and baked or otherwise cooked. It is used to make bread or nan, the large flat or bowl-shaped bread of western Asia, and in central and northwestern India, wheat flour is baked unleavened into chapati. In contrast, in all of Asia to the east of eastern India, the staple food becomes rice, with the whole grains usually boiled or streamed for eating without being ground into flour.

Rice and wheat are thus representative staples of East and West Asia, but the continent also includes peoples who find their staple foods still elsewhere. The varieties of the staple foods of these various ethnic groups are closely linked to the environments in which they live and their own histories. Here, in order to give some thought to the traditional dietary cultures of Asia, let us imagine a map of Asian staple foods as they stood in the 15th century.

On this map, Mongolia to the north and Central Asia are blank because in these areas there was no active agriculture, it being limited to small-scale farming in the oases, and these regions were inhabited by pastoral nomads. For these nomadic peoples, the milk and meat of their livestock were important foods, and they had only such grains as they could procure through trade with the farming peoples to the south.

In the deserts running from southern Iran to the Arabian Peninsula, dates were cultivated in the oases, and the dried dates were an important source of nourishment for those engaging in animal husbandry.

Wheat and barley spread northeast from the ancient seats of West Asian civilization, and a variety of barley suited to cold climates (processed into the parched barley flour called tsampa) also became a staple food in the highlands of Tibet. There barley held sway, while to the east in North China wheat was again the staple diet, where it was made into a kind of steamed bread called mantou or thick wheat noodles.

Various millets--sorghum, German millet, proso millet and the like--were introduced into East Asia from ancient India, long ago passing through the northern mountains of Southeast Asia and on eastward, eventually reaching North China and Manchuria. The ancient Chinese culture that grew up along the Yellow River of North China relied heavily on German millet as its staple. This ancient millet-eating region, however, was later overtaken by the development of cultures whose staple foods were wheat, barley, and rice, and at present, millet remains the sole staple of northern Korea. In India, millet is normally ground and baked as chapati. In North China and Manchuria, it is normally ground, formed into balls, and steamed for consumption, or else the whole grains are boiled into a gruel and eaten. In Southeast Asia, the crops of longest standing are taro, yams, bananas, and others which are not planted as seeds but which are cultivated through transplanting. These, however, were displaced to a major extent by rice and other grains which appeared later, until today the grain-cultivating cultures have taken root in Asia to the extent that the above form the staple diet only in eastern Indonesia and on the islands that dot Bashi Strait between Taiwan and the Philippines. They are still important crops on the islands of Oceania where grain cultivation did not penetrate earlier dietary patterns.

One point that must be made concerning animal proteins deals with the use of milk of domestic animals. In Mongolia in northern Asia, Central Asia, and from India westward, milk from a variety of domestic livestock is made into yoghurt, butter, cheese and other dairy foods, which serve as an important source of nourishment. China, Korea, Japan and Southeast Asia, however, traditionally have not used milk this way. Instead, these non-milk areas developed a variety of fermented foods made from soy beans--for example soy sauce and soy bean paste--and rely heavily on these as sources of vegetable protein in their daily lives.

RELIGION AND DIET

The foods selected for consumption by various ethnic groups and their outlook on food and eating manners are closely related to religion. It is well known that Moslems do not eat pork, but other animals as well must be slaughtered by a Moslem or they cannot be eaten by followers of Islam. The ninth month of the Islamic calendar is a month of fasting, when Moslems may not eat or drink during the daylight hours. For Hindus, the cow is sacred and the eating of beef is forbidden. Many Hindus go further and are vegetarians for religious reasons.

In China, the influence of Taoism has led to the deeply-rooted belief in food as a way to long life. Food is thus deemed to be medicinal, and all foods are classified according to their medicinal properties. For example, eggplant is medicinally effective, it is said, in cooling the blood, so that it should be eaten by those with high blood pressure. Ginger, on the other hand, heats the blood and thus is beneficial to persons with anemia. In this way, a balancing of the condition of the body is sought through food.

In Japan, through the influence of the Buddhist proscription on killing, meat was not commonly eaten until the latter part of the 19th century.

THREE MAIN DIETARY CULTURES OF ASIA

The various peoples of Asia each developed their own ethnic cuisine through the historical interaction of environment and culture. Still, the major civilizations that have appeared in Asia have each exerted an influence on the dietary lives of people of the continent.

Beginning from the west, the three main civilizations would be Persian-Arabian, Indian, and Chinese.

Historically, the food structure of Persian-Arabian civilization began with cooking techniques innovated in ancient Persia and carried forward by Persia during the Sassan Dynasty. With the coming of Islam, to these were added the dietary customs of the Arabs, and through the growth of the Turkish Empire, Turkish methods of cooking were also incorporated in the culinary tradition. In the areas covered by this dietary civilization, nan became widespread, but on special occasions or among the upper classes, the rice dish called pilau was also frequently served. The most important meat was mutton, and a representative food in this region would be the kebab, deriving from Turkish cooking. Another feature is the plentiful use of hot peppers, black pepper, cloves, and other strong spices. Since this is also an Islamic region, the consumption of pork is of course forbidden and other Islamic dietary regulations rule the inhabitants' eating habits. With the spread of Arab culture to North Africa, the cooking practices of Persian-Arabian civilization also advanced into this area, and at the same time, the expansion of the Turkish Empire carried its influence as far as the Balkan Peninsula, the shores of the Black Sea, and Greece.

One characteristic of cooking in Indian civilization has been the daily use of curry in meals. Here, too, through the influence of the Hindu religion, cows are used only for their milk and not for meat. A butter oil called ghee is frequently used in cooking. In addition to rice, chapati made from wheat or barley are also a staple part of the diet, and beans also play an important role in meals.

In Chinese civilization, pork is frequently used, but traditionally the Chinese have not used the milk of their domestic animals. The Chinese also developed the fermented soy bean preparation jiang, primarily in the form of paste or liquid, as a ready-made seasoning. Fats and oils are frequently employed in cooking, and the use of dried and preserved foodstuffs is an other characteristic of Chinese cuisine. The foods, spices, and seasonings go beyond being mere foodstuffs; they are of great importance in cooking based on their classification as medicines for long life. As mentioned earlier, the use of chopsticks and small, individual bowls is also a characteristic of the Chinese cultural sphere.

In Southeast Asia, which has been influenced historically by both Chinese and Indian civilizations, both influences are evident today--the Indian in the curried dishes and the Chinese in the use of a variety of jiang foods and noodles in Southeast Asian cooking.

The arid region stretching from Central Asia to the Caspian sea has been a crossroads not only of culture but of cooking as well. In the oases from Mongolia to Sinkiang, Chinese cooking has made its mark, and Indian cuisine has penetrated to the northwest to reach Pakistan and then Afghanistan, where it has met and intermingled with the foods and methods of preparation of Persian-Arabian culture.

CONTENTS

Char sui cantonese red roasted pork
Lemongrass lamb chops
Miso roasted black cod (misoyaki)
Korean short rib tacos with gochujang sauce
Bun thit noung—lemongrass grilled pork bowl
Naga dog
Tandoori chicken

MY FAVORITE NOODLE DISHES

The last pad thai recipe you'll ever need
My famous drunken noodles
Khao soi northern curry braised beef noodles
Beef pho
Quicker beef pho
Chicken pho (pho ga)
Beef chow fun
Pad see you with chicken
Classic lo mein noodles
Spicy ground pork noodles (dan dan mian)
Japanese noodle bowl (nabeyaki udon—noodles in Pot)
Cold soba noodles with dipping sauce (zaru soba)
Noodle dipping sauce (tsuke—jiru)
Korean chap chae (glass noodles with beef)
Vegan drunken noodles
Vegan pad thai

SOUPS, CURRIES AND LARGER PLATES

Panang chicken curry
Thai green curry with chicken and sweet potato
Hot and sour egg drop soup

Tom yum soup
Coconut chicken soup (tom kha gai)
Red miso soup with tofu
Wonton soup
Deep—fried trout with green mango slaw
Steamed snapper fillet with ginger and scallion
Indian dal (yellow lentils)
Braised vegetable korma

SUSHI, SALADS AND OTHER VEGGIES 149

California roll
Spicy tuna roll
Cucumber kimchi (oi sobagi)
Papaya salad (som tum)
Chicken larb—thai minced chicken salad
Thai beef salad (yum neau)
Coconut mango salad with shrimp
Chilled sesame broccoli salad
Chinese chicken salad
Tofu salad with tangy sesame dressing
Cucumber seaweed salad (sunomono)

DUMPLINGS, FINGER FOODS AND SMALL PLATES 181

Vietnamese crystal shrimp spring rolls
Vietnamese crispy imperial rolls
Vietnamese banh mi sandwich
Sweet chili sriracha hot wings
Thai savory pork jerky (moo dat diow)
Hawaiian og tuna poke
Vegetable and shrimp tempura

Dim sum drum dumpling (sew mai)
Five—spice pork belly sliders
Crab rangoon—cream cheese crab wonton
Sugarcane crispy shrimp
Minced chicken lettuce cups with hoisin sauce

SWEETS: THE TASTIEST WAY TO END ANY DAY

Coconut sticky rice with mango
Fried bananas
Cinnamon and five—spice easy donuts
Green tea ice cream
Ali's coconut rice pudding
8 treasure rice pudding
Thai iced coffee
Homemade instant chai tea mix
Thai iced tea

STOCKS, STAPLES AND BUILDING BLOCKS... 231

Thai chicken stock
Dashi stock
Chinese chicken soup stock
Indian naan bread
Sushi rice
Korean red bean mixed rice
Perfect jasmine rice
Brown rice
Thai sticky rice
Fragrant coconut rice

Bomb-ass homemade sriracha
Grandma's secret hot sauce
Hoisin peanut dipping sauce
Peanut sauce
Vietnamese nuoc cham dipping sauce
Korean gochujang sauce
Sriracha mayo and wasabi mayo
Tempura dipping sauce (tentsuyu)
Teriyaki sauce

ROCK THE WOK
STIR-FRY MASTERY

Yo, don't let that wok scare you into thinking you can't kick its ass! It's a pan, same as the skillet that you've cooked in a thousand times. The only difference is its shape. It's a little deeper, with a rounded bottom sometimes, but that's it. All the principles are the same. You cut your meat and veggies, you prep your seasonings, you get it hot, you add oil and you cook everything until cooked through. And you don't really even need an Asian wok! You have plenty of pans that can do everything a wok can. So cook every recipe in this chapter with a skillet, a fry pan or even a Dutch oven. Actually, a Dutch oven is my favorite wok substitute for the home kitchen. It's heavy with high sides, holds heat amazingly and is flat-bottomed to sit on the stove perfectly.

Remember your yum! Each country tackles the balance of flavor just a little differently. The Chinese all-purpose stir-fry sauce isn't soy sauce, it's oyster sauce. So with Chinese dishes like lo mein, your base sauce will always be oyster sauce. Then add a "plus one" like chili garlic sauce, and you've made Kung Pao. With Thai and Vietnamese dishes like pad Thai and Shaking Beef, your base sauce will always be fish sauce. With Japanese and Korean dishes, your base sauce will be soy sauce. If you know your seasoning starting points with each cuisine, you are on your way to authentic flavors.

Besides seasoning, your other fundamentals are prep and heat control. I'll give you tips in each recipe that will make that recipe awesome. And picking up each tip and practicing will soon make you a black belt in wok cooking. Think about each recipe with its tricks like Daniel-son learning a task from Mr. Miyagi, and soon you'll realize your wok kung fu will start to get amazing. Wok cooking is just like martial arts; anyone can throw a punch or a kick, but the more you do it and understand the nuances, the more your cooking and knowledge improve. And soon you will be beating the shit out of any wok recipes that come your way!

SPICY BASIL BEEF (PAD KRAPOW)

This is one of the most popular street food dishes in Thailand. It's also a technique, kind of like calling something an omelet. An omelet is always egg-based, but you can change the fillings. The base of this dish is always Thai basil, garlic, chilies, bell peppers and onions, but you can switch out the proteins as desired.

SERVES 4

---

3 tbsp (45 ml) sweet soy sauce

2 tbsp (30 ml) oyster sauce

4 tbsp (60 ml) fish sauce

2 tbsp (30 g) chili paste in soybean oil

3 tbsp (45 ml) vegetable oil

3 cloves garlic, minced

1–3 serrano or Thai chilies, sliced

3 cups (720 g) lean ground beef

1 medium onion, sliced

1 small red bell pepper, sliced

1½ cups (335 g) Thai basil leaves, picked off the stem

½ tsp white pepper

Combine the sweet soy sauce, oyster sauce, fish sauce and chili paste in a small bowl and reserve.

Heat your wok or large skillet over high heat and add the vegetable oil. When wisps of white smoke appear, add the garlic and chilies. Cook them until the garlic starts to brown, about 30 seconds.

Stir in the ground beef, flatten against the pan and cook undisturbed for about 45 seconds. The beef will start to brown; turn over once, press flat against the pan and cook for another 30 seconds. Break up the meat into gravel-sized pieces and drain any excess liquid.

Stir in the onion and bell pepper and stir-fry for about a minute. Add the reserved sauce to the wok and combine the ingredients thoroughly for about 1 minute. Add the Thai basil and cook until the beef is thoroughly cooked and onions are slightly tender. Finish with white pepper.

Pro Tip: Substitute any meat or seafood in this dish, which is common in Thailand. Ground chicken or pork are amazing. Top with a runny fried egg or two, and serve over jasmine rice for a perfect meal!

PINEAPPLE FRIED RICE

This is a recipe my family has been serving for 40 years and I've put on every menu I've ever written. I think fried rice is the perfect food. In one plate you get rice, protein, veg and aromatics. What else could you wish for? This is a perfect example of Thai fried rice versus Chinese. Fish sauce is the primary salt, no eggs are used and it's a more wet style of fried rice.

SERVES 4

---

1 large pineapple

3 tbsp (45 ml) vegetable oil

2 tbsp (30 g) dried shrimp (Thai)

4–6 cloves garlic, coarsely chopped

3 tbsp (45 g) diced shallots

½ tbsp (8 g) finely chopped ginger

½ cup (95 g) thinly sliced Chinese sausage

4–6 medium shrimp, peeled and cleaned

4 cups (960 g) day-old rice

2–3 tbsp (30–45 ml) fish sauce

1–2 tbsp (15–30 ml) Thai soybean sauce

1 tbsp (15 g) sugar

½ tbsp (8 g) curry powder

2 to 3 green onions, chopped

Pinch white pepper

3 tbsp (45 g) cilantro leaves

Cut the pineapple in half lengthwise and carve out the middle to create a bowl. Cut about 1 cup (165 g) of pineapple pieces into medium dice and reserve for making the fried rice.

In a large skillet or wok, heat the oil for about a minute or until wisps of white smoke appear. Add the dried shrimp, garlic, shallots, ginger and Chinese sausage and cook, stirring constantly, until the sausage starts to crisp, about 3 minutes.

Stir in the shrimp and cook until the shrimp starts to turn pink, about 1 minute. Fold in the rice, making sure not to break the rice grains. Stir pushing down with the flat side of the spatula in small circular motions. This will separate the grains without breaking them. Cook for an additional minute until the rice starts to get hot.

Stir in the fish sauce, soybean sauce, sugar and curry powder. Continue to stir it for another minute until well combined. Fold in the reserved pineapple and incorporate it well for another 1 to 2 minutes.

Fold in the green onions and white pepper. Transfer the fried rice into the halved pineapple. Garnish with some fresh cilantro.

YANG CHOW FRIED RICE

Fried rice will always be one of my favorite dishes. It was the first dish that my grandmother taught me to make. It's deceptively simple, one of the toughest dishes to make well. Also known as Yangzhou fried rice, from the province of the same name, there are two classic versions. "Silver-covered Gold" technique is cooking the egg first until cooked then tossing in the rice and ingredients after. This is how my grandmother made it when I was a kid. As my career blossomed and I cooked with some masters while in Vegas, I learned the "Gold-covered Silver" technique, where you surround the rice in wet egg and cook it together. I realized this makes the rice light, fluffy and amazing. This dish is the perfect metaphor for my career.

SERVES 4

---

2 tbsp (30 ml) canola oil

2 eggs, beaten

4 cups (450 g) cooked long-grain or jasmine rice, cooled to room temperature

¼ cup (95 g) finely diced cooked Chinese BBQ pork

6 medium shrimp, peeled and cleaned

½ tsp kosher salt

2 tbsp (30 ml) soy sauce

1 tsp powdered chicken bouillon

3 tbsp (45 ml) oyster sauce

½ tsp sugar

2–3 green onions, sliced on the bias

Pinch white pepper

In a large wok or skillet, heat the oil over high heat until a wisp of white smoke appears. Pour in the eggs and add the rice immediately. Using a wide silicone spatula or wooden spatula, work the rice into the egg in circular motions, making sure not to break the rice grains.

After about 30 seconds, the egg will start to coagulate and surround the rice. Add the pork and shrimp and cook until shrimp are almost cooked through, about 1 to 2 minutes. Keep scraping the pan and folding the rice back into the middle.

Add the salt, soy sauce, bouillon, oyster sauce and sugar. Work all the seasonings into the rice until the color is uniform, about 1 minute. Don't be afraid to scrape egg or rice bits stuck to the bottom of the pan. Cook until the rice absorbs the sauces and egg but is still fluffy and moist, about 2 minutes.

Sprinkle on green onions and white pepper and work them gently into the fried rice. Serve immediately.

KIMCHI FRIED RICE

The perfect Asian pub night is multiple rounds of beers, some great dumplings or pork belly buns and a giant plate of Kimchi Fried Rice. The sour and savory flavors of this rich rice are perfect to pair with cold beer. I like using short-grain rice for this because it's extra chewy and pillowy. Short-grain rice is what sushi rice is made from. You'll find kimchi rice in a lot of Japanese pubs, also known as *Izakaya.*

SERVES 4

2 tbsp (30 ml) cooking oil

1 tbsp (15 ml) sesame oil

2 eggs, lightly beaten

3 cloves garlic, coarsely chopped

½ small onion, chopped

4 cups (960 g) day-old cooked short-grain rice

1 cup (240 g) roughly chopped kimchi

½ tsp salt

3 tbsp (45 ml) soy sauce

1 tbsp (15 g) sugar

3 green onions, sliced on the bias

1 tsp white pepper

In a large skillet, heat the oils until a wisp of white smoke appears. Add the eggs and lightly scramble them until just set, about 1 to 2 minutes.

Stir in the garlic and onion, and cook until the onion is translucent, about 1 minute. Fold in the rice and kimchi, pressing down in small circles to separate the rice grains.

Add the salt, soy sauce and sugar. Continue to fold the rice for about 1 to 2 minutes. Don't be afraid to scrape the rice stuck to the bottom of the pan. Cook it for about 1 more minute until the rice absorbs the sauces and is slightly crisp on the edges.

Fold in the green onions and white pepper, cook for an additional minute. Serve immediately.

KUNG PAO SHRIMP

Kung Pao originated from southwest China and is pretty popular in the States. The classic version has peanuts, but I like substituting cashews for their crunch and flavor. A pinch of ground Szechuan peppercorn powder is traditional. Add it if you have it, but you'll be fine without it! Also, you can substitute any meat, seafood or tofu for the shrimp.

SERVES 4

2 tbsp (30 ml) Chinese chili garlic sauce, more if you like it hot

⅓ cup (90 ml) oyster sauce

1 tsp sesame oil

¼ cup (60 ml) chicken stock or water

1 tsp cornstarch dissolved in 1 tsp water

3 tbsp (45 ml) vegetable or canola oil

3 cloves garlic, chopped

4–6 dried chili de arbol (or similar)

3 lb (1.3 kg) medium shrimp, about 21–25, peeled and deveined

1 red bell pepper, cut like French fries

1 medium onion, cut into large dice

⅔ cup (150 g) whole roasted cashew nuts

Pinch white pepper

Pinch of Szechuan peppercorn powder

3 green onions, sliced on the bias

In a small bowl, combine the chili garlic sauce, oyster sauce, sesame oil, chicken stock and cornstarch slurry and set aside.

Heat a large sauté pan or wok over high heat for about a minute. When you see the first wisps of white smoke, swirl in the oil, garlic and chilies. Stir and scrape until the garlic is light brown, about 30 seconds.

Toss the shrimp into the pan and stir constantly until the shrimp just starts to turn pink and everything starts to smell amazing, about 1 more minute. Stir in the vegetables and nuts, and cook for about a minute, until the onion starts to turn translucent.

Add the sauce, Szechuan peppercorn powder, pinch of pepper, and stir everything in the pan together until the sauce coats the shrimp and thickens. Cook for an additional minute or until the shrimp are cooked through.

Sprinkle in the green onions, give it a good stir, and enjoy.

Pro Tip: Szechuan peppercorn or peppercorn powder is easy to find on the Internet. Also known as "prickly ash," it has an amazing flavor that's a cross between white pepper and pine. It also has the fun effect of making your tongue tingly and a little numb. If you can't find it, leave it out; this recipe is still super tasty!

MONGOLIAN BEEF

This is another American-born Chinese dish that is part of our wok vocabulary. I will always firmly believe that dishes, like Mongolian beef and California roll, that were born in the States are authentic dishes. The secret to tender meat in the wok is the marinade. You will see this in many of my recipes. Baking soda tenderizes the meat, cornstarch and water create a slurry that brings in the baking soda and oil pre-lubricates the meat and keeps us from using too much oil in the wok.

SERVES 4 TO 6

Beef

1½ lb (750 g) flank steak, trimmed

1 tsp baking soda

1 tsp salt

2 tbsp (16 g) cornstarch

2 tbsp (30 ml) water

2 tbsp (30 ml) vegetable oil

Sauce

1 tsp minced garlic

1 tsp minced ginger

3 tbsp (45 ml) oyster sauce

3 tbsp (45 ml) hoisin sauce

2 tbsp (30 ml) soy sauce

3 tsp (16 ml) white vinegar

½ tbsp (4 g) cornstarch

Stir-Fry

3 tbsp (45 ml) vegetable oil

3 cloves garlic, minced

4–6 dried chilies

½ red bell pepper, cut into large dice

½ green bell pepper, cut into large dice

½ medium onion, cut into large dice

2 green onions, sliced

Slice the flank steak across the grain into ¾-inch (19 mm)-thick slices on an angle to make planks then cut the planks into ¾-inch (19 mm) cubes. Place the steak in a shallow bowl and add the baking soda, salt, cornstarch, water and vegetable oil. Massage all the ingredients into the meat. Set it aside until ready to use, or you can cover and refrigerate for a few days.

Combine all sauce ingredients and set aside.

Heat the oil to medium high in a wok or medium sauté pan, and sauté the garlic until light brown. Stir in the beef and allow to cook undisturbed for about 30 seconds. Stir and scrape the pan and cook for another 30 seconds. Stir in all the vegetables and let them cook for about 2 minutes, until the onion starts to turn translucent.

Add the sauce, stir constantly and let it cook for about 2 minutes, until the sauce thickens.

Stir in the sliced green onions and serve.

CARAMEL SHAKING BEEF

This is my version of the classic Vietnamese dish. The shaking is what you are doing to the pan while cooking. It's the motion of moving the pan back and forth to marry the beef with the sticky, sweet, salty sauce. Maggi is a branded sauce that's widely available. It's basically a soy sauce fortified with sugar and other seasonings. If you can't find it, you can use any soy sauce.

SERVES 4 TO 6

---

2 lb (900 g) boneless beef sirloin, tenderloin or rib eye, cut into 1" (2.5-cm) cubes

10 cloves garlic, minced, divided

1 tbsp (15 ml) fish sauce

2 tbsp (30 ml) Maggi seasoning sauce

3 tbsp (42 g) sugar

1 tbsp (15 ml) vegetable oil

2 tbsp (28 g) butter

Pinch freshly ground black pepper

1 loaf crusty French bread

In a bowl, combine the beef, half of the garlic, fish sauce, Maggi and sugar. Let the mixture stand at room temperature for about half an hour. It's a good idea to turn your hood fan on as this dish will smoke a bit.

Preheat a wok or large skillet over high heat for about 2 minutes. When hot, pour in the vegetable oil. The pan will start to smoke, immediately pour in the marinade and beef AWAY from you to avoid oil splatter. Start to move the pan back and forth to keep the beef searing and moving. Add the remaining half of the minced garlic and keep moving until the beef is seared on all sides but still medium rare, about 1 minute. Drop in the butter and shake for another minute to finish. The butter will melt and combine with all the delicious juices in the pan and make a phenomenal pan sauce!

Platter the beef and all the pan sauce, sprinkle with freshly ground black pepper. Serve with crusty bread to sop up all that deliciousness.

GENERAL TSO'S CHICKEN

There's been a lot of rumor about the origins of this dish; I'll let others fight it out and just focus on its deliciousness! I think that the human palate is drawn to the combination of savory, sour, sweet, salty and spicy. I think that's why we all love this dish. There's a huge difference between the popular sambal oelek and Chinese chili garlic sauce. Sambal is very easy to find but it's twice as hot as chili garlic. So, if you are using sambal, use half the amount.

SERVES 4

Sauce
½ cup (90 ml) oyster sauce

1 tbsp (15 ml) hoisin sauce

1 tbsp (15 ml) chili garlic sauce

½ cup (95 g) sugar

3 oz (90 ml) white vinegar

2 tbsp (30 ml) soy sauce

½ tbsp (8 g) minced ginger root

½ tbsp (5 g) chopped garlic

1 tbsp (7 g) cornstarch mixed with 1 tbsp (15 ml) water

1 drop red food coloring (optional)

Chicken
1½ qt (1.8 L) vegetable oil, plus 2 tbsp (30 ml) for stir-frying

2 lb (900 g) boneless chicken thighs, cut into 2″ (5-cm) dice

1½ cups (335 g) tempura flour, plus

1 cup (223 g) for dredging

1 cup (240 ml) cold water

½ onion, cut into large dice

10–12 whole dried Thai chilies

1½ cups (335 g) broccoli florets, steamed in microwave for 1 minute

3 scallions, sliced on the bias

For the Sauce

Add all the sauce ingredients into a 1-quart (946-ml) saucepan, and bring the heat up to medium. Whisk gently as it comes to a simmer. Allow it to simmer and keep whisking it for about 5 minutes, until the sauce thickens. Remove from the heat and reserve it.

For the Chicken

Heat the oil in a 4-quart (3.8-L) Dutch oven to 375°F (190°C) using a frying thermometer. Rinse the chicken in cold water and pat dry with paper towels. Mix 1½ cups (335 g) of the tempura flour and 1 cup (240 ml) water into a thick batter. It should look like thick pancake batter. Dredge the chicken cubes in 1 cup (223 g) of tempura flour and fry them in two batches until golden brown and crispy, about 6 to 8 minutes. Drain the chicken on paper towels or a rack.

Heat a wok or large skillet to high and add 2 tablespoons (30 ml) of oil. When you see the first wisps of white smoke, stir in the fried chicken, onion, chilies and broccoli and cook them for about 30 seconds. Stir in the sauce and allow it to coat the chicken and simmer. Cook it, folding all the ingredients until they are well coated, about 2 minutes. Garnish with scallions.

SALT AND PEPPER SHRIMP

This is the classic Cantonese shrimp dish with the heads and shells left on the shrimp. I know this is scary for some. The recipe is left traditional, but you can substitute peeled shrimp if you prefer. I think the shells and head hold the seasoning perfectly. You can choose your own adventure here, but I hope you try this dish as it was meant to be eaten.

SERVES 4

---

2 tsp (10 g) kosher salt

1 tbsp (30 g) chicken bouillon powder

½ tsp white pepper

2 tbsp (60 g) finely chopped scallions

1 tsp sugar

1½ lb (600 g) large shrimp, unpeeled

1 cup (115 g) cornstarch

2 qt (1.8 L) vegetable oil for deep frying plus 2 tbsp (30 ml) for stir-frying

2 tbsp (20 g) finely chopped garlic

1 tbsp (10 g) minced ginger

1 red jalapeño pepper, sliced thin, with seeds

In a small bowl, combine the kosher salt, bouillon powder, white pepper, scallions and sugar and reserve.

Rinse the shrimp under cold water, drain them quickly in a colander, but leave them moist to absorb the cornstarch to make a crust.

Heat the oil in a 6-quart (5.7-L) Dutch oven or pot until the oil reaches about 375°F (190°C). Place the cornstarch in a large bowl, dredge the shrimp in cornstarch and then shake off the excess. Deep-fry the shrimp for 2 to 3 minutes in three small batches. Drain on a sheet pan as you are heating your skillet or wok.

While the shrimp are cooking, heat a large skillet or wok to high. Spoon in 2 tablespoons (30 ml) of oil. When the first wisp of white smoke appears, stir in the garlic, ginger and jalapeño and cook for about 30 seconds until light brown.

Toss in the fried shrimp and reserved sugar-and-salt mixture. Continually toss the shrimp to coat well, about 1 to 2 minutes. Once the shrimp are heated through, plate the shrimp and top with crispy bits from the pan.

 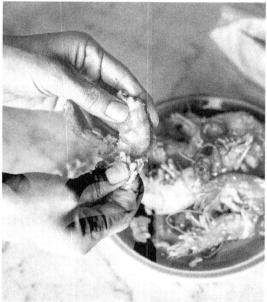

ORANGE-FLAVORED CHICKEN

OK, you can judge me all you want, but you know you love orange chicken! You might call it junk food, but we all need to indulge sometimes! I've been trying to figure out this recipe for years. I think the gold standard of this dish is from that restaurant that has the black-and-white bear, you know the one. But I've finally cracked the code and here you go! If you don't want to make the nuggets from scratch, similar items are pretty easy to find in the frozen section in the market.

SERVES 4

Sauce

½ cup (118 ml) oyster sauce

1 tbsp (15 ml) hoisin sauce

3 oz (90 ml) orange juice

½ cup (95 g) sugar

3 oz (90 m) white vinegar

2 tbsp (30 ml) soy sauce

½ tbsp (8 g) ground paprika

½ tbsp (4 g) minced ginger root

2 cloves garlic, minced

1 tbsp (7 g) cornstarch mixed with 1 tbsp (15 ml) water

1 drop red food coloring (optional)

Chicken

1½ qt (1.8 L) plus 2 tbsp (30 ml) vegetable oil, divided

2 lb (900 g) chicken thighs, cut into 2" (5-cm) dice

1 cup (240 ml) cold water

1½ cups (335 g) tempura flour plus

1 cup (223 g) for dredging

½ onion, cut into large dice

4 scallions, sliced into 2" (5-cm) lengths

For the Sauce

Add all the sauce ingredients into a 1-quart (946-ml) saucepan, and bring the heat up to medium. Whisk gently as it comes to a simmer. Allow it to simmer, and keep whisking for about 5 minutes until the sauce thickens. Remove from heat and reserve.

For the Chicken

Heat 1½ quarts (1.8 L) oil in a 4-quart (3.8-L) Dutch oven to 375°F (190°C) using a frying thermometer. Rinse the chicken in cold water and pat it dry. Mix the tempura flour and water into a thick batter. It should look like thick pancake batter. Dredge the chicken cubes in 1 cup (223 g) of tempura flour roll in a thin layer of the batter and fry them in two batches until golden brown and crispy, about 6 to 8 minutes. Drain the chicken on paper towels or a rack.

Heat a wok or large skillet to high and add 2 tablespoons (30 ml) of oil. When you see the first wisps of white smoke, stir in the fried chicken, onion and scallions and cook for about 30 seconds. Stir in the sauce and allow it to coat all the ingredients and simmer. Cook, folding all the ingredients until they are well coated, about 2 minutes. Serve over hot rice.

BEEF AND BROCCOLI

Do not think this is just a Chinese American classic! Do think this is delicious, is quick to cook and will make you a kitchen hero. This dish was originally made with Chinese broccoli, and I would recommend that you make it that way sometime. You can also use this recipe as a guide to make veggies and beef.

SERVES 4

1 lb (450 g) broccoli florets

1 tbsp (15 ml) soy sauce

1 tsp sesame oil

2 tsp (4 g) cornstarch, divided

1 tsp baking soda

1 lb (450 g) flank steak

⅓ cup (80 ml) beef or chicken stock

2 tsp (10 ml) rice wine

¼ cup (60 ml) oyster sauce

2 tbsp (30 ml) vegetable oil

2 cloves garlic, minced

Blanch the broccoli in boiling salted water for about 2 minutes or until slightly tender and dark green. Shock it in ice water and drain thoroughly.

In a small bowl, whisk together the soy sauce, sesame oil, 1 teaspoon cornstarch and baking soda. Slice the beef against the grain into thin strips and add it to your marinade. Let it sit for at least 20 minutes, or as long as overnight in the refrigerator.

In a separate small bowl, stir together the stock, rice wine, oyster sauce and remaining 1 teaspoon cornstarch until the cornstarch is fully dissolved.

Heat a wok or a large skillet on high heat and add the oil. When a wisp of white smoke appears, toss the marinated beef and garlic into the pan. Cook for about a minute, continually moving the beef so it browns on all sides but is still rare. Once the beef is seared, add the broccoli and cook for an additional minute. Stir in the sauce and keep it all moving. Don't be afraid to scrape any bits off the bottom of the pan before they start to burn. Once the sauce has turned into a nice thick glaze, about 1 minute, serve immediately.

Pro Tip: Like a lot of my stir-fry dishes, break them up into three parts to simplify. Get in the habit of marinating your meats before cooking. This makes them super tender and they will feel and taste just like your fave Chinese restaurant's. Then combine the sauces into one bowl. All that's left is to stir-fry!

MORNING GLORY ON FIRE

Morning glory, aka ong choy, aka water spinach, is a staple vegetable in many asian countries. It's crisp, delicious, nutritious but most of all makes you look like a BAMF in the kitchen when stir-frying it up! There's a famous street food vendor in Bangkok who cooks this dish fired in the wok on one side of the street, then hurls it across the street at his partner, who catches it on a plate and serves it tableside. You can substitute your favorite greens like spinach or broccoli for the morning glory.

SERVES 4

3 tbsp (45 ml) vegetable oil

3 cloves garlic, finely chopped

2 lb (900 g) ong choy (morning glory), washed and cut into 4" (10-cm) lengths

2 tbsp (30 ml) yellow bean sauce

3 tbsp (45 ml) oyster sauce

1–2 Thai chili peppers, thinly sliced

Heat the oil on high in a large pan or wok for about 1 minute. When you see the first wisps of white smoke, sauté the garlic until golden brown, about 30 seconds.

Add the morning glory, yellow bean sauce, oyster sauce and chili peppers. Keep it all moving, constantly folding and scraping the bottom. Stir-fry for about 2 to 3 minutes or until the morning glory is slightly tender and bright green.

Serve immediately.

Pro Tip: Yellow bean sauce is a Thai sauce made from fermented soybeans, like soy sauce. In soy sauce, the soybeans are fully fermented until black. Yellow bean sauce is made with soybeans that are partially fermented and not mashed.

SZECHUAN BEEF

Although I specified flank steak for this recipe, filet mignon is an amazing choice! It cooks and eats like butter, super tender. This is a drier stir-fry, meaning there's not a lot of natural gravy. If you love a ton of sauce, you can always add about ¼ cup (60 ml) of chicken stock with 1 teaspoon of water and 1 teaspoon of cornstarch. Add this slurried stock at the end, and you'll have delicious gravy with every bite.

SERVES 4

___

Szechuan Sauce

3 tbsp (45 ml) oyster sauce

1 tbsp (15 ml) chili garlic sauce

1 tbsp (15 g) sugar

1 tsp sesame oil

1 tsp Szechuan peppercorn powder

½ tsp chili flakes

¼ tsp salt

Szechuan Beef

2 tbsp (30 ml) peanut or canola oil

1 lb (450 g) flank steak, 3″ (7.6-cm) julienne against the grain

2 tsp (10 g) minced ginger

2 cloves garlic, minced

2 tsp (10 ml) Shaoxing rice wine or sherry

3 celery ribs, 3″ (7.6-cm) julienned

2 scallions, cut into 2″ (5-cm) lengths

For the Sauce

In a small bowl, combine the sauce ingredients, and reserve.

For the Szechuan Beef

Heat your wok or large skillet to high and add the oil. Distribute the oil evenly using a spatula. When a wisp of white smoke appears, stir in the beef, ginger and garlic, and cook for about 1 minute or until the beef is medium rare.

Add the rice wine or sherry and deglaze the pan. Let the alcohol burn off and absorb into the beef. Fold in the sauce and stir well to coat the beef.

Add the celery and cook it for 20 to 30 seconds, or until just tender. Then add the scallions and cook for an additional minute or until heated through.

SWEET AND SOUR PORK WITH PINEAPPLE

Sweet and sour isn't just an Americanized Chinese dish. It has a deep history in China. It's from Hunan and started simply as sauce that was made with vinegar and sugar. The most famous version is from Hong Kong, and this is my version of that sauce. If you are freaked out by the food coloring, just leave it out. But it adds visual appeal to the dish.

SERVES 4

Sweet and Sour Sauce

3 tbsp (45 ml) water

4 tbsp (50 g) sugar

1 drop red food coloring (optional)

3 tbsp (45 ml) vinegar

½ cup (90 ml) ketchup

3 tbsp (45 ml) Worcestershire sauce

1 tbsp (7 g) cornstarch mixed with

1 tbsp (15 ml) water to make a slurry

Pork

1½ qt (1.8 L) vegetable oil, for deep-frying plus 2 tbsp (30 ml) for stir-frying

2 lb (900 g) pork loin or shoulder, cut into 2″ (5-cm) dice

1½ cups (335 g) tempura flour plus

1 cup (223 g) for dredging

1 cup (240 ml) cold water

1 onion, cut into large dice

1 red bell pepper, cut into large dice

1 (20-oz [567-g]) can pineapple chunks, drained

3 scallions, thinly cut on the bias

For the Sauce

Add all the sauce ingredients into a 1-quart (946-ml) saucepan and bring the heat up to medium. Whisk gently as it comes to a simmer. Allow it to simmer and keep whisking for about 3 minutes, until the sauce thickens. Remove the sauce from the heat and reserve it.

For the Pork

Heat the oil in a 4-quart (3.8-L) Dutch oven to 165°F (74°C) using a frying thermometer. Rinse the pork in cold water and pat it dry. Mix the tempura flour and water into a thick batter. It should look like thick pancake batter. Dredge the pork cubes in 1 cup (223 g) of tempura flour, roll in a thin layer of batter and fry it in two batches until it's golden brown and crispy, about 6 to 8 minutes. Drain it on paper towels or a rack.

Heat a wok or large skillet to high and add 2 tablespoons (30 ml) of oil. When you see the first wisps of white smoke, stir in the fried pork, onion, red bell pepper and pineapple and cook them for about 30 seconds. Stir in the sauce and allow it to coat and simmer. Cook, folding the ingredients, until they're all well coated, about 2 minutes. Garnish with scallions.

SZECHUAN-STYLE GREEN BEANS

This technique for the beans is called twice cooking. The Chinese flash-fry items to precook them then finish in a wok. Think about it like blanching broccoli or beans just to take the raw flavor out of things and jumpstart the cooking process since wok cooking is so fast. I like wok cooking and deep-frying in any high-temp low-flavor oil. Vegetable, corn, canola or soybean oils are my favorite. If you want to get fancy, grapeseed is also a great one. I'd set up a large Dutch oven for the first fry. Use about 4 inches (10 cm) of oil. While you are frying your beans, have your wok heating up so you can stir-fry immediately.

SERVES 4

Sauce

2 tbsp (30 ml) hoisin sauce

2 tbsp (30 ml) oyster sauce

2 tbsp (30 ml) Chinese rice wine or dry sherry

1½ tbsp (22 g) brown sugar

1 tsp chili garlic sauce

Green Beans

1 lb (450 g) green beans, trimmed

4 cups (960 ml) canola or peanut oil

1¾ cups (200 g) cornstarch for dredging

2 tbsp (30 g) Tianjin preserved vegetable or any Chinese preserved vegetables (optional)

2 tbsp (20 g) chopped garlic

2 tbsp (18 g) chopped ginger

For the Sauce
Combine the sauce ingredients in a small bowl and set aside.

For the Green Beans
Wash the green beans and drain them thoroughly.

Add the oil to a deep skillet and bring the oil temperature up to 375°F (190°C). Dredge the beans in the cornstarch in a large bowl, knocking off any excess.

Deep-fry the beans for 1 to 3 minutes, until their skins begin to wrinkle but they're still crisp. Remove from the oil and drain on paper towels.

Heat a separate deep skillet or wok to high and add 2 tablespoons (30 ml) of the oil leftover from deep frying. When you see a few wisps of white smoke, stir in the preserved vegetables, garlic and ginger and brown for 30 seconds or until fragrant. Add the beans to the pan, folding constantly for about 30 seconds. Stir in the sauce and fold into the beans until well combined. Cook for about 1 minute until all the ingredients are thoroughly combined.

SPICY PORK WITH PEANUTS

Western China is warm, rich and fertile and grows the country's best chilies. So it's no mystery why dishes like Kung Pao and Szechuan come from there. Peanuts are a new-world ingredient that probably originated in or around Brazil. They were brought to China and also grow in this region. I created this dish because it captures everything I love about the area.

SERVES 4

Sauce

3 tbsp (45 ml) oyster sauce

1 tbsp (15 ml) chili garlic sauce

1 tbsp (15 g) sugar

1 tsp sesame oil

6–8 whole dried chilies

¼ tsp salt

Pork

2 lb (900 g) pork shoulder or loin

1 tsp baking soda

1 tsp salt

2 tbsp (15 g) cornstarch

2 tbsp (30 ml) water

2 tbsp (30 ml) vegetable oil

1 tbsp (15 ml) canola oil

2 cloves garlic, finely minced

6 oz (180 g) green bell peppers, batonnet-cut

8 oz (240 g) red bell peppers, batonnet-cut

8 oz (240 g) onions, batonnet-cut

⅓ oz (10 g) dried red chili peppers

2 oz (50 g) dry-roasted peanuts

For the Sauce

Combine all the sauce ingredients and set aside.

For the Pork

Slice the pork across the grain into ¼-inch (6-mm) thick slices on an angle. Place the pork in a shallow bowl and add baking soda, salt, cornstarch, water and vegetable oil. Massage all the ingredients into the meat to combine. Set it aside until ready to use, or you can cover and refrigerate for a few days.

Heat the canola oil to medium high in a wok or medium sauté pan. When you see the first wisps of white smoke, sauté the garlic until light brown. Stir in the pork and allow it to cook undisturbed for about 30 seconds. Stir and scrape the pan and cook for another 30 seconds. Stir in the bell peppers, onion, red chilies and peanuts and cook them for about 2 minutes, until the onions start to turn translucent.

Add the sauce, stir constantly, and let it cook for an additional minute until the ingredients are piping hot and combined. Serve immediately.

CALIFORNIA FRIED RICE

This is a great vegan fried rice recipe. Soybean sauce is Thailand's version of soy sauce. It has a sweeter, more savory flavor than the Japanese version. You can also use Maggi seasoning sauce, which has the same flavor and is easy to find. Vegetarian oyster sauce can also be found online and is a great substitute for oyster sauce.

SERVES 2 TO 4

2 tbsp (30 ml) cooking oil

2 cloves garlic, coarsely chopped

4 cups (960 g) day-old cooked brown rice

½ cup (95 g) shelled edamame

¼ cup (50 g) frozen peas and carrots

⅓ cup (85 g) tofu, cut into medium dice

2 tbsp (30 ml) Thai soybean sauce (Maggi or Golden Mountain brand)

2 tbsp (30 ml) vegetarian oyster sauce (optional)

Pinch salt

½ tbsp (8 g) sugar

2–3 green onions, chopped

Pinch white pepper

In a large skillet or wok, heat the oil until a wisp of white smoke appears. Stir in the garlic and cook until it's light brown, about 30 seconds. Fold in the rice, edamame, peas and carrots and tofu, pressing down in small circles to separate the rice grains. Stir in the soybean sauce, vegetarian oyster sauce, salt and sugar; fold until all ingredients are incorporated. Don't be afraid to scrape any rice or bits stuck to the bottom of the pan. Cook it until the rice absorbs the sauces and is slightly crisp on the edges, about 1 minute.

Fold in the green onions and white pepper and cook the rice for an additional minute.

BUDDHA'S DELIGHT—VEGETABLE FEAST

There are times when I just crave a wok full of vegetables, and this is my go-to dish. It's chock full of different textures and flavors. If there is something you hate, get rid of it and sub in something you love! This is a light, healthy but super flavorful vegetable stir-fry.

SERVES 4

Sauce
⅓ cup (90 ml) vegetable stock
3 tbsp (45 ml) oyster sauce
1 tbsp (15 ml) soy sauce
½ tsp brown sugar
1 tsp sesame oil
1 tsp cornstarch
Pinch white pepper

Vegetable Stir-Fry
2 tbsp (30 ml) vegetable oil
1 (14-oz [420-g]) package firm tofu, cut into large dice
2 tsp (10 g) thinly sliced ginger
12 cremini mushrooms, sliced
4 oz (95 g) canned sliced bamboo shoots
6 canned water chestnuts, sliced
1 cup (240 g) bean sprouts
½ cup (120 g) julienned carrots
1 cup (240 g) shredded Napa cabbage leaves
2 oz (95 g) snow peas, trimmed

For the Sauce
Stir together all the sauce ingredients in a small bowl, making sure the cornstarch is dissolved well. Set aside.

For the Vegetable Stir-Fry

Heat a wok or a large skillet over medium-high to high heat. Swirl in 2 tablespoons (30 ml) of oil to the heated wok and coat the bottom. When you see wisps of white smoke, add the tofu, and stir-fry until light brown on the edges, about 2 minutes. Then add the ginger and stir-fry it until aromatic, about 30 seconds. Add all the remaining vegetables and keep them moving while searing. Don't be scared to scrape the pan and fold the vegetables over many times. Cook for about 1 to 2 minutes or until the Napa cabbage gets bright green and starts to soften.

Stir in the sauce, coat all the vegetables and tofu, and bring the sauce to a boil. The cornstarch will thicken into a glaze, about 1 minute. Remove from heat and serve immediately.

Pro Tips: Cut all the larger vegetables into ¼-inch (6-mm) strips and keep smaller vegetables like snow peas and beansprouts whole.

The best tofu for the wok is tofu that is vacuum packaged, not the tofu in water. This tofu has naturally formed a skin and will not stick in the wok or pan. It comes naturally white, fried or often coated in a soy sauce or five-spiced glaze. It is usually in the deli section of a well-stocked grocery store and sometimes merchandised next to the cheese and cold cuts. Tofu in water should only be used for wet applications like soups or braises.

GRILLING, ROASTING AND MORE MEAT

My favorite type of cookery is definitely meat cooking. These are some of my favorite dishes to eat and cook. From classics like satay and BBQ chicken to my own creations, like Korean Tacos, you will love them all.

Cooking meat and seafood perfectly is an art and one of my favorite things to do. You see a lot chefs striving to get that perfect color and temperature from every piece of meat. You see them squeezing and poking their meat to identify the perfect doneness. All that takes a lot of time to learn and understand. Here are some of my favorite tips and tricks that will help you bend that learning curve to your favor. Keep in mind, grilling doesn't just mean an open wood or gas fire; it also applies to a stove and grill pan.

Always preheat your grill, give it a dry brush to remove debris and then lubricate just like you oil a pan. This will help give you a great sear mark. Remember there's only one presentation side, so work at making it look killer! If it looks delicious and the temp is right on, you have won the battle! The only way to accurately tell doneness will always be temperature. Here are your meat temps:

Beef medium rare is 125°F (52°C) and every 10 degrees above is a doneness level.

Lamb medium rare is 145°F (53°C).

Chicken has to be cooked to 165°F (74°C) always.

Carryover cooking is the phenomenon of the meat temperature continuing to rise after being removed from heat. The higher the cooking heat and the larger the piece of meat, the more it will carryover. Assume 2 to 5 degrees for small pieces of meat being grilled, and 10 to 15 for large pieces cooked for longer periods.

Try bringing your meat to room temperature before cooking; this will help with even cooking. If you grill your meat right out of the fridge, it won't cook through evenly. You'll burn the exterior before the middle gets to the target temp. Let marinades do their job of penetrating the meat. Give them time to work and wipe off excess before cooking to keep the meat from burning. With the words of wisdom above, you are well on the way to grilling like a boss!

THAI BBQ CHICKEN WITH SWEET CHILI SAUCE

The secret to moist, tender evenly cooked Thai BBQ chicken is roasting in the oven, then finishing on the grill. Trying to grill chicken from raw will make you want to poke your eye out. Roasting the bird in halves cooks it evenly while locking in the juices and intensifying the marinade flavors. It also takes the guess work out of wondering if you cooked the bird to a safe temp. Roast until the internal temp is 165°F (74°C), rest and you can grill to get those marks and flavor after.

MAKES 8 PIECES OF CHICKEN

1 (3½-lb [1.6-kg]) chicken

2 tbsp (30 g) minced ginger root

2 tbsp (8 g) minced lemongrass

1 tbsp (3 g) minced cilantro leaves and stems

2 cloves garlic, minced

2 tsp (10 g) white pepper

¼ cup (60 ml) thin soy sauce

1 tbsp (15 g) sugar

2 tbsp (30 g) curry powder

1 cup (240 ml) coconut milk

Sweet chili sauce for dipping

Split the bird in half lengthwise. Poke holes in the chicken using a fork and place into a gallon-size (3.8-L) zippy bag. Combine the remaining ingredients, except the sweet chili sauce, in a blender and blend them until smooth.

Pour the marinade mixture over the bird and coat it evenly. Close the bag and massage the bird well. Zip up the bag tight and let the chicken marinate in the fridge for at least 4 hours to overnight.

Preheat the oven to 375°F (191°C) and place a rack just below the middle. Lay the chicken halves skin-up on a foil-lined sheetpan and bake for about 45 minutes or until a thermometer reads 160°F (71°C) in the fleshy part of the thigh. Pull from the oven and rest for at least 10 minutes. You can cut each half into 4 and serve! You can also grill to get some marks and favor. Always serve with sweet chili sauce!

SALMON TERIYAKI

This is a staple recipe in my house. My pantry is always stocked with the basics like soy and mirin. If you don't have sake on hand, feel free to sub it out for sherry or white wine. Teri means "glaze" or "sauce" and yaki means "grill." Traditionally a piece of fish would be grilled over hardwood charcoal and then glazed with a luscious sauce that's sweet, salty and very savory. This version would be a Japanese home-cook version where all the work is done in one pan. I'm a believer that you can make better sauces than store bought. This teriyaki sauce recipe can be multiplied, shaken together in a bottle and held in the fridge until ready to use.

SERVES 4 TO 6

Teriyaki Sauce

2 oz (60 ml) sake

3 oz (90 ml) mirin

4 oz (120 ml) soy sauce 3 tbsp (45 g) sugar

1 tbsp (8 g) cornstarch combined with 1 tbsp (15 ml) water

Salmon Teriyaki

2 lb (910 g) salmon filets, boned and scaled, cut into 3" (8-cm) pieces

Salt and pepper

2 tbsp (30 ml) vegetable oil

For the Teriyaki Sauce

Mix all the ingredients in a small saucepan and bring to a simmer over medium heat; whisk about 1 to 2 minutes until the sugar dissolves and the sauce bubbles and thickens slightly. Set it aside to use on the salmon, and store any leftovers in the refrigerator.

For the Fish

Pat the fish dry with a paper towel and season it with salt and pepper.

Heat the vegetable oil in a medium-sized, heavy-bottomed skillet over medium-high heat. Once you start to see white smoke, lay the filets skin-side down in the skillet. Move the fish around constantly while cooking to keep it from sticking. When the fish is medium, about 4 to 6 minutes, turn with a spatula only once.

Cook the other side for another minute. Add the Teriyaki Sauce to the pan and reduce the heat to low. The sauce will begin to simmer and reduce. Tilt the pan around a few times and turn the fish until it's well coated with the sauce.

Remove the fish to individual plates. Continue to heat the remaining sauce and stir for a minute or so to deglaze the pan and give the sauce luster. Spoon a few tablespoons of this sauce over the fish.

STREET VENDOR PORK SATAY

Satay, in its most popular form, originated in Java, Indonesia, but many of us food historians believe it has its roots in the Arab shish kebab. Over many centuries, Arabs made their way up to India and eventually into the West Indies. It's such a great dish because it picked up a little of each culture along the way. The practice of skewered and roasted dishes comes from the Mideast. Turmeric came from the spice traders. Peanuts came from the New World and were carried to Asia. I love this Thai version the best because of its variety and depth of flavor.

MAKES ABOUT 10 TO 12 SKEWERS

---

1 tbsp (15 g) curry powder

½ tbsp (8 g) pepper

1 tbsp (15 g) salt

1 tbsp (15 g) sugar

1 tsp garlic powder, or more to taste

¼ cup (60 ml) coconut milk

2 lb (900 g) pork shoulder or pork loin

10 to 12 (6″ [15-cm]) bamboo skewers, soaked

Peanut Sauce, for serving

To make the marinade, combine the curry powder, pepper, salt, sugar, garlic powder and coconut milk in a medium bowl.

Slice the pork against the grain into 2-inch (5-cm) square tiles about ¼-inch (6-mm) thick. Add to the marinade and massage to coat it evenly. You can cook immediately or marinate overnight for better flavor and tenderness. Thread the pork onto the bamboo skewers, leaving 2 inches (5 cm) at the bottom of each skewer.

Heat a grill or griddle to high and preheat for at least 5 minutes. Rub a little oil on the grill or spray with pan spray to lube the grill. Grill the pork for about 3 to 5 minutes on the first side or until you get a nice brown. Flip and cook for another 3 to 5 minutes until just cooked through. Serve with Peanut Sauce.

KOREAN BBQ SHORT RIBS ON COKE

This is the classic Korean BBQ recipe with a twist. I was taught that the secret to tender grilled short ribs is using apple pear and Coca-Cola©. Both help break down the beef. That classic thin 3-bone piece of short rib is called flanken cut. If you can't find it at an Asian market, tell any butcher you want ½-inch (1.3-cm) thick flanken cut short ribs. KBBQ pros like myself love a slightly chewy texture, but it's not for all. If that makes you cringe a little, use any steak cut of beef, like flank, NY strip or even rib-eye. This recipe is perfect by itself or served with rice or rice-and-grain blends. Add some Gochujang or chili sauce and the recipe gets spicy.

SERVES 4

¼ cup (60 ml) soy sauce, I prefer regular but low sodium is fine

¼ cup (60 ml) Coca-Cola© soda

3 tbsp (40 g) brown sugar, packed

2 cloves garlic, finely minced

½ apple pear, grated

1 tbsp (15 ml) toasted sesame oil

2 lb (907 g) flanken-cut short ribs

2 green onions, very finely sliced on an angle

1 tbsp (12 g) toasted sesame seeds

Combine the soy sauce, Coke, brown sugar, garlic, apple pear and sesame oil in a large bowl. Using a whisk or fork, stir all the ingredients until the sugar is dissolved and garlic is distributed evenly. Add the short ribs and massage the marinade into the beef. Cover and allow the short ribs to marinate for 1 to 4 hours.

Heat a grill or pan to high for at least 5 minutes. If using a charcoal or gas grill, wipe the grill grates down with a lightly oiled towel right before cooking to clean any char and debris. This will give you a great grill mark and help keep the beef from sticking.

Pat any marinade off the short ribs and grill for about 4 minutes on each side or until desired doneness. Remove from the grill and garnish with green onions and sesame seeds.

BULGOGI—SESAME BEEF

One of the classic Korean BBQ dishes, this is also very useful for adding a Korean beef to other dishes, like bibimbap, or making mash-up dishes like Korean tacos and quesadillas. The secret to hand slicing into paper-thin slices is to freeze the meat until semi-solid, about 3 hours. It will still be pliable but very firm. You can also buy the beef presliced at any Korean market. This marinade is also great for making a Korean-style rib eye, NY strip or filet mignon.

SERVES 4

1½ lb (675 g) rib-eye beef

¼ cup (450 ml) soy sauce

1 tbsp (15 ml) sesame oil

1 tbsp (15 ml) sesame seed, toasted

3 cloves garlic, finely minced

3 tbsp (45 g) granulated sugar, brown sugar or honey

2 green onions, sliced

¼ cup (45 ml) water

2 tbsp (30 ml) vegetable oil for cooking

Slice the beef ⅛-inch (3-mm) thick, and then cut it into little bite-size pieces.

Place all the remaining ingredients, except the water, in a large bowl and mix them together until the sugar is dissolved.

Add ¼ cup (60 ml) of water to the mixture, stir and add the beef. Let it set for at least 3 hours or overnight.

Heat a large skillet to high and add the oil. When you see a wisp of white smoke, add the meat to the pan. Let sear for about 1 minute until brown. Turn the beef slices over and sear for an additional 1 to 2 minutes, until the beef is browned but still medium rare. Serve immediately.

KOREAN SPICY GRILLED CHICKEN

Gochujang is a sticky, sweet, hot Korean chili paste. I think it's the most balanced, delicious chili paste in all of Asia. It has sweet, smoky and savory notes that other sauces lack. Sriracha has been all the rage for so long, but in my humble opinion, gochujang kicks sriracha's ass!

SERVES 4

Marinade
¼ cup (450 ml) soy sauce

1 tbsp (15 ml) sesame oil

½ cup (95 g) gochujang

1 tbsp (15 ml) sesame seeds, toasted

3 cloves garlic, finely minced

3 tbsp (45 g) granulated sugar, brown sugar or honey

¼ cup (45 ml) water

Chicken
2 lb (900 g) chicken thighs

2 green onions, sliced

For the Marinade
Place all the marinade ingredients together in a large bowl and whisk together until fully combined.

Roll the chicken thighs in the marinade, cover and allow to marinate for 2 hours to overnight, the longer the better.

For the Chicken

When ready to cook, remove the chicken from the marinade and place on a foil-lined sheet. I like roasting these in the oven at 375°F (190°C) for about 30 minutes, until the internal temperature is 165°F (74°C), and finishing it on the grill. You can also grill these over indirect heat for about 25 minutes until browned with the same internal temperature. Garnish with green onion.

CHAR SUI CANTONESE RED ROASTED PORK

This is that classic Cantonese red roasted pork you see in restaurants and hanging in the windows of barbecue shops. I like using pork butt, which isn't butt or rump at all but shoulder, for its fat content. If you really love a leaner, less fatty cut, loin is a better choice. This dish can also be used in the Yang Chow Fried Rice and for making BBQ pork buns.

SERVES 4

Marinade
2 tbsp (30 ml) sherry

1 tbsp (25 g) minced ginger root

⅓ cup (80 ml) oyster sauce

½ tsp Chinese five-spice powder

4 oz (85 ml) soy sauce

¼ cup (50 g) white sugar

3 oz (90 ml) hoisin sauce

3 oz (90 ml) ketchup

Pork
2 lb (900 g) pork butt

4 tbsp (60 ml) honey

2 drops red food coloring (optional)

For the Marinade

In a large bowl, stir together the sherry, ginger, oyster sauce, five-spice powder, soy sauce, white sugar, hoisin sauce and ketchup. Set aside.

For the Pork

Preheat the oven to 350°F (175°C). Cut the pork into 6-inch (15-cm) long by 3-inch (8-cm) wide strips. Place the strips flat in a shallow baking dish. Pour the marinade over the pork strips. Let the pork marinate overnight in the refrigerator.

Drain the pork, reserving the marinade in a small saucepan. Stir in the honey and food coloring until completely combined. Bring to a boil and reserve for basting and plating.

In your oven, position one rack on the bottom and the other about 5 inches (13 cm) above it. Place a shallow roasting pan on the bottom rack, add water to the pan until three-quarters full. Carefully place the pork strips on a roasting rack above the roasting pan so all sides of the pork strips are exposed to heat.

Roast the pork for 30 minutes. Baste the pork strips with the honey mixture. Roast for 15 minutes and baste again. Roast for 10 minutes longer or until the pork strips are crisp and golden brown. Remove from the oven and let cool. To serve, slice into ½-inch (1.25-cm) strips and smother with reserved sauce.

LEMONGRASS LAMB CHOPS

I think a lot of folks are a little intimidated by the thought of cooking lamb chops at home. The perception is that lamb doneness is hard to nail perfectly, and it has some kind of natural funk and you need magic seasoning to make it delicious. Both are total BS by the way. Plus it's one of those wow-your-friends-and-family dishes. Here are the hacks to perfect lamb chops. Have your butcher cut the rack into chops so they look clean. Marinate the chops for a few hours and make sure to wipe the excess before cooking so you don't burn them. Lastly, it's essential to use a meat thermometer to check doneness. Once you hit 145°F (63°C), pull out the chops and rest them for at least 5 minutes. If you follow these three rules, you will be hailed a kitchen god by your friends and family!

SERVES 4

2 tbsp (50 g) peeled and roughly chopped lemongrass

1 tbsp (15 g) finely chopped kaffir lime leaves (lime zest can work too)

2 tbsp (30 g) roughly chopped shallot

3 cloves garlic, minced

½ tbsp (3 g) coriander powder

1 tbsp (6 g) curry powder

1½ tbsp (45 g) sugar

½ tsp salt

2 cups (500 ml) coconut milk

4 lb (1.8 kg) lamb rib chops

Peanut Sauce or sweet chili sauce for serving

Simply combine all of the ingredients except the lamb in a blender and pulse until well puréed. Place the lamb in a large bowl, pour the marinade over, and massage it in for about 30 seconds. Cover the bowl with plastic and marinate the lamb chops for at least 2 hours in the fridge. This is a good recipe to prep the night before.

Heat a grill or skillet to high and preheat for a minute. Remove the lamb from the marinade and wipe off a little of the excess with a paper towel. Rub the grill or pan with a little vegetable oil. Sear very well on one side until you get a beautiful brown, about 4 minutes. Turn over and cook for an additional 3 minutes or until the internal temperature is 145°F (63°C). Rest for 5 to 10 minutes and serve with Peanut Sauce or sweet chili sauce.

Pro Tip: Don't worry about cutting the herbs perfectly for this; they are going in a blender anyway.

MISO ROASTED BLACK COD (MISOYAKI)

Black cod is the pork belly of the ocean. Pleasantly fatty, super savory and pretty bulletproof to cook. What makes this dish extra delicious is a technique called laminating or sugar brining. We make a miso sauce that's sweet and savory and submerge the fish in it for a few days. The moisture in the fish gets replaced with the miso sauce. The fancy chemistry term is equilibrium.

SERVES 4 TO 6

---

1 cup (240 ml) sake

1 cup (240 ml) mirin

3 oz (85 g) granulated sugar

3 oz (85 g) brown sugar

1 lb (450 g) white or yellow miso

3 tbsp (75 g) grated ginger

2 lb (900 g) black cod fillet, scales removed

Preheat a 2-quart (1.9-L) saucepan over high heat for about a minute and add the sake. Bring it to a boil to cook off the alcohol. Careful, the sake might ignite. Stir in the mirin, both sugars, miso and grated ginger and bring to a boil. Reduce the heat to a simmer, and cook the marinade for about 5 minutes, until it turns a pale caramel color. Remove from the heat and allow it to cool completely. Separate out ¾ cup (120 ml) of the marinade to use for basting later.

Cut the fish into 6-ounce (170-g) pieces, leaving the skin on. Place the fish pieces in a shallow baking dish, pour the marinade over the fish until it is completely submerged. Marinate overnight or up to 2 days.

Place an oven rack about 12 inches (30 cm) from the broiler. Remove the fish from the marinade and wipe all excess marinade off the fillets. Line a baking sheet with foil, spray the foil with cooking spray and lay the fish on the foil. Broil for 10 to 12 minutes or until lightly brown on top and cooked through.

The fillets will have shrunk a bit and pin bones should be sticking out slightly. Pull out the pin bones and discard them. To finish, drizzle some of the reserved marinade on the fish and broil again until golden brown.

Pro Tip: Due to its richness and soft texture, the common name of black cod in Hawaii is butterfish. The secret to getting the perfect brown color is twice cooking.

KOREAN SHORT RIB TACOS WITH GOCHUJANG SAUCE

I think the most famous food truck mash-up dish is the Korean taco. This is my version using braised short ribs. It's also a two-fer recipe: the braised short ribs are delicious on their own, but using my short ribs to make a Korean taco is kind of like taking a tank to a fistfight! It's so over-the-top delicious. I'm calling it here and now, gochujang is going to be the next super popular chili sauce and will replace sriracha as the king of spicy sauces. It's sweet, savory, smoky and hot. It's the perfect hot sauce; you can use it on anything!

MAKES ENOUGH FOR 12 TACOS

Braised Short Ribs
½ cup (100 g) all-purpose flour

1 tbsp (16 g) kosher salt

1 tsp cracked pepper

4 lb (1.8 kg) beef short ribs

¼ cup (50 g) butter, divided

2 shallots, chopped

3 cloves garlic, chopped

½ lb (225 g) onion, cut into large dice

¼ lb (100 g) carrot, cut into large dice

¼ lb (100 g) celery, cut into large dice

1 (750-ml) bottle dry red wine

2 sprigs fresh thyme

1 bay leaf

1 sprig flat-leaf parsley

4 cups (946 ml) beef broth

Korean Taco Sauce
¼ cup (60 g) gochujang

⅓ cup (67 g) sugar

⅓ cup (80 ml) soy sauce

1 tbsp (15 ml) sesame oil

Tacos

2 lb (900 g) sliced Brussels sprouts

½ cup (75 g) chopped onion

Salt and pepper

12 small corn tortillas

2 limes, cut into wedges

For the Braised Short Ribs

Preheat the oven to 325°F (165°C).

Combine the flour, salt and pepper in a large bowl. Dredge the beef in the seasoned flour and shake off the excess; set aside. Heat 2 tablespoons (30 g) of butter in a 4- or 5-quart (3.8- to 4.8-L) Dutch oven over high heat. Brown the short ribs on all sides, about 10 minutes.

Melt another 2 tablespoons (30 g) of butter in the pan. Stir in the shallots, garlic, onion, carrot and celery. Cook and stir until the vegetables have softened, about 10 minutes. Add the wine and reduce it by half. Stir in the thyme, bay leaf, parsley and beef broth. Place the browned short ribs on top of the vegetables in a single layer, and then bring it to a boil.

Cover it with a tight-fitting lid or aluminum foil, then bake it in the preheated oven until the short ribs are very tender and nearly falling off the bone, about 3 to 3½ hours. Once the short ribs are tender, strip the meat off the bone with a fork and place in a serving dish. Cover and keep warm.

For the Korean Taco Sauce

Whisk all the sauce ingredients together until the sugar has dissolved and the mixture is smooth. You can make this a few days in advance and store it tightly covered in the refrigerator.

To Assemble the Tacos

Sauté some of the shredded short rib with Brussels sprouts, onions, salt and pepper to prepare the taco filling. Heat some of the tortillas on the grill. Spoon ½ cup (120 g) of the taco filling into each tortilla. Serve it with the Korean taco sauce and a lime wedge.

BUN THIT NOUNG—LEMONGRASS GRILLED PORK BOWL

You usually think about pho when going to a Vietnamese restaurant, but it's time to graduate to bun! Bun is a type of noodles, made of rice like pho but thinner and springier. They are cooked, chilled and then used as a base for cold noodle bowls. My favorite protein to top these bowls with is this delicious sweet, smoky lemongrass pork. I love cooking this on a hot griddle to get a great sear.

SERVES 4

Nuoc Cham Dipping Sauce
2 tbsp (30 ml) lime juice

¼ cup (60 ml) fish sauce

¼ cup (60 ml) water

1 tbsp (15 ml) rice vinegar

¼ cup (50 g) sugar

1 garlic clove, minced

1 Thai chili, finely chopped

Pork
2 shallots, sliced thin

2 cloves garlic, minced

1 tbsp (30 g) minced lemongrass

2 tbsp (30 g) water

3 tbsp (45 g) granulated sugar

3 tbsp (45 ml) fish sauce

Heavy pinch black pepper

1 lb (450 g) pork butt, sliced paper-thin against the grain

2 tbsp (30 ml) vegetable oil

8 oz (240 g) Vietnamese thin rice sticks (bun)

Assembly

½ cup (95 g) shredded daikon radish

½ cup (95 g) shredded carrot

3 tbsp (45 g) coarsely chopped roasted peanuts

3 scallions, thinly sliced

For the Dipping Sauce

Combine all the sauce ingredients and stir to dissolve the sugar completely. Set aside.

For the Pork

Combine all of the marinade ingredients in a blender; purée about 20 seconds until smooth. Place the pork in a medium bowl, pour the marinade over the meat and massage the pork well. Marinate for at least 1 hour. Heat a medium skillet to high and add the oil. When you see white wisps of smoke, sauté the pork for about 5 minutes until cooked through.

For the Noodles

Boil the rice sticks in 3 quarts (2.8 L) of water in a 4-quart (3.8-L) pot for about 12 minutes until al dente. Rinse them well under cold water in a fine mesh strainer and reserve.

Assembly

Divide the noodles into 4 separate bowls. Place the pork on top of the noodles. Sprinkle the pork with radish, carrot, roasted peanuts and scallions. Pour Nuoc Cham Sauce over the noodles, and mix them well like a salad.

NAGA DOG

Modern food truck food is a great mashup of cuisines. This Japanese mashup is a perfect way to make a hot dog interesting for BBQs, tailgates or just when you need to change up hot dog night. Try these sauces on your favorite burger as well!

MAKES 4 DOGS

4 red hot sausages

4 hot dog buns

4 oz (113 g) Wasabi Mayo

4 oz (113 g) Sriracha Mayo

½ cup (100 ml) Teriyaki Sauce

¼ cup (180 g) kimchi

4 tbsp (60 g) shredded nori seaweed

Warm the hot dogs and buns on a flat top until cooked through. Load the link into the bun. Start by slathering 1 ounce (28 g) each of the Wasabi and Sriracha Mayo, then 1 ounce (28 ml) Teriyaki Sauce. Top the dog with kimchi and nori shreds.

TANDOORI CHICKEN

The amazing thing about Indian food is the mastery of spices. Marinating in yogurt makes the chicken here super tender and juicy. The combo of spices and herbs really makes the chicken sing. Tandoors cook food at well over 800 degrees, like the hottest pizza ovens. To achieve that at home, I like to get a charcoal grill crazy hot by getting the maximum load of briquettes to their peak of heat. Load them on one side of the grill, cover and let that heat build up. Cook over indirect heat until you get a beautiful brown and the chicken is just cooked through.

SERVES 4

2 lb (900 g) boneless chicken thighs, skins removed

1–2 tsp (5–10 g) salt

2 lemons, juiced

1¼ cups (300 ml) plain yogurt

½ onion, grated with the large holes of a box grater

1 clove garlic, minced

2 tsp (10 g) grated ginger root

2 tsp (10 g) garam masala

1 tsp cayenne pepper

1 tsp paprika, for color

2 tsp (10 g) finely chopped cilantro

1 lemon, cut into wedges

Cut small slits in the chicken thighs with a paring knife to allow the marinade to penetrate. Place them in a shallow dish. Sprinkle both sides of the chicken with salt and lemon juice. Set it aside for 10 minutes.

In a medium bowl, combine the yogurt, grated onion, garlic, ginger, garam masala and cayenne pepper. Mix them until smooth. Stir in the paprika. Spread the yogurt mixture over the chicken. Cover it, and refrigerate for 6 to 24 hours (the longer the better).

Preheat your grill to medium-high heat, and lightly oil the grates. Cook the chicken on the grill for about 6 minutes on each side until beautifully brown, or until internal temperature is 165°F (74°C) degrees. Garnish it with cilantro and lemon wedges.

Pro Tip: I've written this recipe for chicken thighs but it's very versatile. It's great for legs, breasts, even wings. This recipe is also great for fish. Tandoori halibut is amazing. And grilling can be a pain, so feel free to roast your tandoori in a super-hot oven. Heat your oven to 500°F (260°C), line a baking sheet with foil and spray with a little oil. Place your tandoori on the oiled foil and cook away!

MY FAVORITE NOODLE DISHES

If you love noodles, this is your chapter! It's loaded with some of my all-time bests. Buying this book just for my <u>Drunken Noodles</u>

might have been worth it, but the pad Thai, lo mein and khao soi? I should have spread all those classics between four books. Cook through this chapter and you'll have a great feel for the traditional Asian approach to cooking noodles and seasoning them.

An important tip for this chapter is to always use the right noodle from the country the dish is from. Making pad Thai with ramen noodles makes no sense, and your guests will feel the same way. You don't have to be a culinary expert to know when something isn't right. Experience is your expertise. Eating pad Thai and/or Ramen a few hundred times makes you an expert enough. Noodles can be categorized a million ways, and unlike Italian food, Asians don't categorize by shape. Know that most noodles are made with wheat, rice or starch. They can be kneaded, steamed, extruded or rolled. They can be pan-fried, deep-fried, steamed or boiled. I think it's important to study the dishes and make sure you do all you can to find the right noodle.

THE LAST PAD THAI RECIPE YOU'LL EVER NEED

The most famous Thai dish in America! Making a good pad Thai takes time. There's a delicate dance with the noodles because they cook in three stages. First you soak them in warm water and they begin to absorb water and soften. In the pan, they first get pan-fried with all the ingredients. Be patient in this stage. Allow them to begin to yield and marry with the hot oil and other ingredients. Once they look soft enough to eat right out of the pan but are slightly al dente, add the sauce to finish their cooking.

My family was among the first to introduce this dish to America over 40 years ago, and the American version differs slightly from the native one. The super bright orange was accentuated with paprika instead of the traditional addition of chili paste to give it a slight tint. And we typically finish this dish with garlic chives versus green onions. I always say pad Thai is like pancakes. You'll burn a few before you get the knack for it.

SERVES 4 TO 6

Pad Thai Sauce
4 tbsp (60 ml) Thai fish sauce

3 tbsp (45 ml) bottled tamarind paste

1 tbsp (15 ml) lime juice

1 tbsp (15 ml) rice vinegar

4 tbsp (50 g) sugar

Pad Thai
2 tbsp (30 ml) vegetable oil

2 cloves garlic, minced

2 tbsp (30 g) packaged shredded sweetened radish

1 tsp dried shrimp

½ cup (95 g) sliced baked tofu

2 eggs

½ cup (95 g) thin strips of chicken breast or thigh

10 large shrimp, peeled and cleaned

3 cups (750 g) medium rice sticks, soaked

2 tsp (10 g) paprika

3 green onions cut into 3″ (8-cm) julienne

¼ cup (50 g) chopped dry-roasted unsalted peanuts, divided

1 cup (240 g) bean sprouts

For the Pad Thai Sauce

To make the sauce, combine the fish sauce, tamarind paste, lime juice, vinegar and sugar in a small bowl. Make sure to stir well until the sugar dissolves, then reserve.

For the Pad Thai

Heat a skillet or wok over high heat for about 1 minute or until the pan gets pretty hot. Add the oil and swirl to coat the pan completely. When the pan just starts to smoke, add garlic and stir about 5 seconds. Add radish, dried shrimp and tofu and stir-fry until they begin to get fragrant, about 1 minute.

Push the ingredients in the wok to one side and let the oil settle in the center of the pan. Crack the eggs into the pan and add the chicken. As the eggs start to fry, just pierce the yolks to let them ooze. Fold the chicken and eggs over for about 30 seconds or until the eggs begin to set and scrape any bits that are starting to stick. Now stir together to combine all the ingredients in the pan.

Add the shrimp and allow to cook for about 30 seconds until they just start to turn color and become opaque. Add the soaked (and drained) rice noodles and cook for about 2 to 3 minutes until soft. Add the reserved sauce mixture and paprika and fold together until the paprika evenly colors the noodles and all the liquid is absorbed, about 2 minutes.

Place the green onions in the center of the noodles, and then spoon some noodles over the green onions to cover and let steam for 30 seconds. Stir in 3 tablespoons (38 g) of the peanuts. Transfer to a serving plate and garnish with bean sprouts and the remaining peanuts.

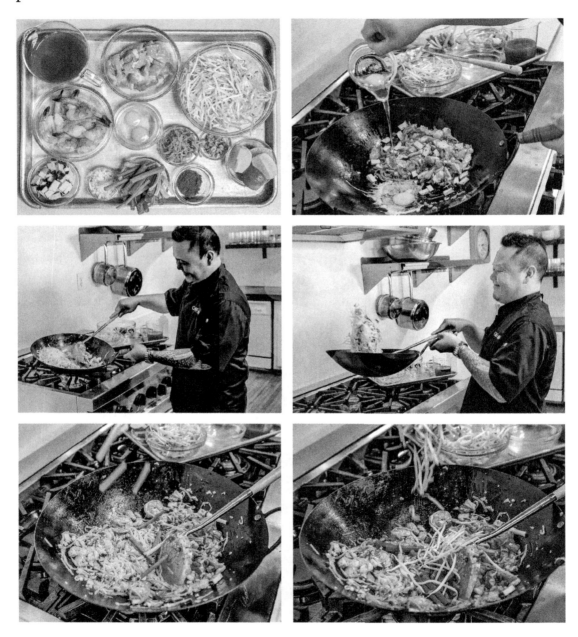

MY FAMOUS DRUNKEN NOODLES

Famous for being a late night drinking dish, Drunken Noodles is a marriage between my Thai and Chinese roots. The sauce seems complicated, but it's as simple as measuring and dumping in a bowl. Fresh rice noodles are a deli item at most Asian markets. They are made and delivered fresh daily to the markets. It's best to buy and use them within 48 hours. A way to tell if they are fresh is just to take the pack and fold it like a towel. If you can fold until the ends touch and the middles aren't cracking, that's a sign of freshness.

SERVES 2 TO 4

Sauce

2 tbsp (30 ml) sweet soy sauce

1 tbsp (15 ml) oyster sauce

1½ tbsp (22 ml) fish sauce

1 tbsp (15 g) sugar

1 tsp Sriracha

1 tsp minced garlic

6–8 Thai basil leaves, chiffonade

Noodles

3 tbsp (45 ml) canola or peanut oil

2–3 cloves garlic, minced

2 eggs

1–2 serrano chilies, sliced thin

6–8 large shrimp, peeled and deveined

½ medium white onion, sliced

4 cups (960 ml) fresh rice noodles, separated

1 cup (40 g) Thai basil leaves, loosely packed

½ cup (75 g) grape tomatoes, halved

For the Sauce

Combine the sauce ingredients in a small bowl and set it aside.

For the Noodles

In a large sauté pan, heat the oil over high heat. When you see a wisp of white smoke, add the garlic and sauté until it's light brown.

Add the eggs and serrano chilies in and lightly scramble the eggs until they're barely set, about a minute.

Add the shrimp, onions and tomatoes, folding constantly until the shrimp turn pink, about 1 minute.

Add the fresh rice noodles, basil leaves and sauce and toss to combine for about 3 minutes. Don't be scared to scrape the bits off the bottom before they burn. Cook for 1 minute until the noodles are cooked and coated well. Finish by tossing in the basil and grape tomatoes, allowing them to lend their flavors. Cook for about an additional minute and serve hot.

KHAO SOI NORTHERN CURRY BRAISED BEEF NOODLES

This is hands-down my favorite noodle dish to eat and cook. It comes from my mom's home region of northern Thailand. This dish is very reminiscent of the popular Japanese tonkotsu ramen. The coconut curry is fortified with a very rich broth. Khao is the Thai word for rice, in this case rice noodles, and soi means "to cut." So this dish was originally made with hand-sliced rice noodle sheets, but the modern version is adapted for thin wheat noodles.

SERVES 4

4 cups (960 ml) coconut milk, separating the top 3 tbsp (45 ml) of cream

2 tbsp (30 ml) yellow curry paste

2 tbsp (30 ml) masamun curry paste

2 kaffir lime leaves, cut into a fine chiffonade

½ cup (90 ml) rich beef stock

2 tsp fish sauce

1 tbsp (15 ml) tamarind paste

1 tsp sugar

1 lb (450 g) Braised Short Ribs

½ lb (240 g) fresh flat egg noodles, boiled until al dente

½ cup (90 g) Chinese pickled mustard greens, drained and sliced thin

½ cup (90 g) shallots, peeled and cut in small dice

4 scallions, sliced on the bias

Cilantro leaves for garnish

In a medium saucepan, heat 3 tablespoons (45 ml) of the thick coconut cream on high for about 1 minute. When the cream starts to sizzle, stir in the curry pastes like building a roux, and add the lime leaves. Stir-fry the paste for about 1 minute, until the paste starts to thicken, dry out, and become fragrant. If the curry starts to sputter, add a small amount of coconut milk to keep the paste moving. Stir in the remaining coconut milk into the curry paste. Increase the heat to high until you reach a full rolling boil. Allow the curry to boil for about 5 to 10 minutes or until it reduces by about a quarter or coats the back of a wooden spoon.

Reduce the sauce to a simmer add the rich beef stock, fish sauce, tamarind and sugar. Taste and adjust as necessary. Add the short rib meat at the last possible moment before serving; it will only take about a minute for the meat to warm and absorb the luscious curry broth.

Divide the noodles into 4 bowls. Ladle about 6 to 8 ounces (177– 237 ml) of the rich broth over each noodle bowl, and make sure each bowl gets a few slices of beef. Garnish with mustard greens, shallots, scallions and cilantro.

Pro Tip: Use my braised short rib recipe here for the meat in this curry noodle dish. Save the rich stock from that braise for the broth.

BEEF PHO

Beef Pho is quickly gaining popularity in America. Its rich aromatic broth is satisfying but not heavy and it eats clean. It also has everything you want in one bowl: the broth, tender pieces of braised beef, vegetables and aromatics. Remember to cook a nice large piece of roast in the stock, which you'll slice later for the dish.

MAKES 4 QUARTS (3.8 L) BROTH

3 lb (1.4 kg) marrow bones or oxtails

1 large onion, halved

2 (4″ [10-cm]) pieces ginger root

6 qt (5.7 L) water

2 lb (910 g) chuck roast

6 star anise

3 whole cloves

1 cinnamon stick

⅓ cup (80 ml) Vietnamese fish sauce

3 oz (85 g) sugar

Salt

½ lb (240 g) rice stick noodles, cooked, drained and cooled

½ lb (240 g) reserved roast (slightly frozen and sliced paper thin)

1 onion, sliced paper thin

4 scallions, sliced

½ cup (95 g) cilantro leaves

½ lb (200 g) bean sprouts

½ cup (95 g) Vietnamese basil

2 jalapeño chilies, sliced thin

2 limes, cut into wedges

Sriracha and hoisin sauce for serving

Preheat your oven to 475°F (246°C). Line a roasting pan with foil and spray it with oil. Place the bones, onion halves and ginger on that sheet and roast for 25 to 40 minutes or until all the ingredients are nicely browned; do not burn. Remove from the heat and reserve.

Add 6 quarts (5.7 L) of water to a large stockpot. Add the chuck roast, roasted bones, ginger and onion. Turn the heat up to high and let the water temperature rise gradually, this will keep the stock from getting too scummy and cloudy. Once the water starts to boil, reduce to a simmer. Simmer for about 2 hours skimming any foam and fat off the surface every 20 minutes.

Wrap the star anise, cloves and cinnamon stick in a piece of cheesecloth and tie into a bundle with butcher twine (we call this a sachet). Simmer the sachet in the broth for 45 minutes. Stir in the fish sauce and sugar until completely incorporated; salt to taste. Taste the broth for the spices, and if it's not strong enough, simmer for 10 more minutes. Repeat this until you are happy. When happy, remove the sachet from the broth. Cooking the spices too long will make the broth dark and too pungent.

Remove the roast from the pot and soak it in cold water until it's cooled through. Wrap it in plastic to prevent drying and darkening. Refrigerate until you are ready to serve it.

Strain the broth and hold it until you are ready to use.

Distribute the noodles among 4 bowls. Top with some sliced beef, onion, scallions, cilantro, bean sprouts, basil and jalapeños. Bring the broth to a simmer and ladle in enough to cover the ingredients in the bowl. Garnish with a lime wedge. I like to serve pho with Sriracha and hoisin sauce.

QUICKER BEEF PHO

I wrote this recipe for fast pho because you don't always want to take a whole day to source the ingredients and make pho from scratch. This is an awesome hack to be eating pho in an hour! You can find all the ingredients locally and even have them delivered. Slicing beef paper thin can be a pain. Japanese and Chinese markets always stock paper-thin meats for shabu shabu or sukiyaki.

MAKES 2 LARGE OR 4 SMALL BOWLS

Pho Stock
1 qt (960 ml) water
2 tbsp (30 g) beef bouillon or base
1 (2″ [5-cm]) piece ginger, sliced into thin tiles
½ onion, sliced thin
1 tbsp (15 g) Vietnamese fish sauce
1 tbsp (15 g) white sugar
2 whole star anise
2 whole cloves
1 cinnamon stick
Pinch kosher salt

Assembly
½ lb (240 g) rice stick noodles, cooked, rinsed and drained
½ lb (240 g) beef strip loin or fillet, shaved thin
1 onion, sliced paper thin
4 scallions, sliced thin on the bias

½ cup (95 g) cilantro leaves

1 cup (240 g) bean sprouts

½ lb (240 g) Vietnamese basil

5 jalapeño chilies, sliced thin

1 lime, cut into wedges

Sriracha and hoisin sauce for serving

For the Stock

Add the water and beef base to a 2-quart (1.9-L) saucepan and bring to a boil. Add the ginger, onion, fish sauce and sugar to the stock and reduce to a simmer. Wrap the star anise, cloves and cinnamon stick in a piece of cheesecloth and tie it into a bundle. Let the bundle simmer in the broth for no more than 45 minutes. Stir in the salt and check the seasonings. Strain and reserve.

To Assemble

Distribute the noodles among 4 bowls. Top with some sliced beef, onion, scallions, cilantro, bean sprouts, basil and jalapeños. Bring the broth to a simmer and ladle in enough to cover the ingredients in the bowl. Garnish with a lime wedge. I like to serve pho with Sriracha and hoisin sauce.

CHICKEN PHO (PHO GA)

My wife likes chicken pho more than beef, and I know lots of peeps who just don't eat beef. Browning chicken bones before making stock is a great way to concentrate flavors and gives a depth to the stock you can't achieve normally. This technique is technically called a brown stock (versus a white stock) and is key to this soup.

MAKES 4 QUARTS (3.8 L) BROTH

---

3 lb (1.3 kg) chicken bones and wings

1 large onion, halved

1 (4″ [10-cm]) piece ginger, sliced into thin planks

6 qt (5.7 L) water

2 lb (900 g) chicken breast

6 star anise

3 cloves

1 cinnamon stick

⅓ cup (80 ml) Vietnamese fish sauce

3 oz (85 g) sugar

Salt

½ lb (240 g) rice stick noodles, cooked, drained and cooled

½ lb (240 g) reserved chicken breast, slightly frozen and sliced paper thin

1 onion, sliced paper thin

4 scallions, sliced

½ cup (95 g) cilantro leaves

½ lb (200 g) bean sprouts

½ cup (95 g) Vietnamese basil

2 jalapeño chilies, sliced thin

2 limes, cut into wedges

Sriracha and hoisin sauce for serving

Preheat your oven to 475°F (246°C). Line a roasting pan with foil and give it a spray with oil. Place the bones, onion halves and ginger on that sheet and roast for 25 to 40 minutes or until all the ingredients are nicely browned; do not burn. Remove from the heat and reserve.

Add 6 quarts (5.7 L) of water to a large stockpot. Add the roasted bones, ginger and onion. Turn the heat up to high and let the water temperature rise gradually; this will keep the stock from getting too scummy and cloudy. Once the water starts to boil, reduce to a simmer. Simmer for about 1 hour, skimming any foam and fat off the surface every 20 minutes. Now add the whole chicken breast to the stock.

Wrap the star anise, cloves and cinnamon stick in a piece of cheesecloth and tie into a bundle with butcher twine (this is called a sachet). Simmer the sachet in the broth for 45 minutes. Stir in the fish sauce and sugar until completely incorporated; add salt to taste. Taste the broth for the spices; if not strong enough, simmer for 10 more minutes. Repeat this until you are happy. When happy, remove the sachet from the broth. Cooking the spices too long will make the broth dark and too pungent.

Remove the chicken breast from the pot and soak it in cold water until cooled through. Wrap it in plastic to prevent drying and darkening. Refrigerate until you are ready to serve it. Strain the broth and hold it until you are ready to use.

Distribute the noodles among 4 bowls. Top with some sliced chicken, onion, scallions, cilantro, bean sprouts, basil and jalapeños. Bring the broth to a simmer and ladle in enough to cover the ingredients in the bowl. Garnish with a lime wedge. I like to serve pho with Sriracha and hoisin sauce.

BEEF CHOW FUN

Fun isn't just what you feel cooking from this book; it's the Chinese word for fresh wide flat noodles. Technically this recipe is a "dry" chow fun, meaning there's very little gravy in the dish. There's also a version that creates a ton of sauce.

SERVES 4 TO 6

8 oz (240 g) flank steak, fat and connective tissue trimmed

¼ tsp baking soda

1 tbsp (15 ml) Chinese black soy sauce

1½ tbsp (12 g) cornstarch

4½ tbsp (66 ml) vegetable oil, divided

2 slices ginger, julienned

2 cloves garlic, finely minced

1 lb (450 g) fresh wide rice noodles (hor fun), separated

4 oz (112 g) bean sprouts, rinsed and drained

2 scallions, cut into 2" (5-cm) sections

4 tbsp (60 ml) oyster sauce

3 tbsp (45 ml) Chinese black soy sauce

Slice the flank steak across the grain into ¼-inch (6-mm) thick slices on an angle to make thin planks. Place the steak in a shallow bowl and add baking soda, soy sauce, cornstarch and 1½ tablespoons (22 ml) vegetable oil. Massage all the ingredients into the meat to combine. Set it aside until ready to use or you can cover and refrigerate for a few days.

Heat a wok or large skillet over high heat until you see the first wisp of white smoke. Add 1 tablespoon (15 ml) of the oil, the ginger and the garlic to the wok. Stir-fry them for about 15 to 30 seconds, until fragrant. Carefully add the beef, spreading it in the wok. Cook, undisturbed, for 30 seconds to 1 minute, letting the beef begin to brown. Then stir-fry 1 to 2 minutes, or until the beef is browned but still slightly rare.

Add the remaining 2 tablespoons (30 ml) of oil to the wok with the noodles, spreading around to cover as much surface area as possible. Cook undisturbed for about 30 seconds or until slightly crisp on the edges. Add the bean sprouts and stir-fry them for an additional minute or until fragrant and tender. Add the scallions, oyster sauce and black soy and stir-fry 1 to 2 minutes, or until heated through and well combined. If you love a saucy noodle dish, stir 2 teaspoons (6 g) of cornstarch mixed with ¼ cup (60 ml) of chicken stock into the finished noodles before removing from the heat.

Pro Tip: Hor fun, or fresh Chinese rice noodles, can be found in the tofu area of most Chinese or Thai markets. You can also use extra-large dried rice stick noodles for this dish. Soak them in warm (180°F [82°C]) water for about 45 minutes and sub them right into the recipe.

PAD SEE YOU WITH CHICKEN

Americans might eat pad Thai or drunken noodles, but pad see you is the most popular Thai noodle dish for Thais. It has a smoky, sweet and savory flavor that is truly addicting. Sweet soy sauce is an ingredient you need to get acquainted with ASAP! It's used heavily in China, Indonesia and Malaysia. It's really just Chinese-style soy sauce mixed with molasses—pretty darn simple and delicious! Not very salty, it's more sweet and savory, and it's the key to making delicious pad see you. Pad means to stir-fry. See you translates to "soy sauce" in Thai, similar to shoyu in Japanese.

SERVES 4

3 tbsp (45 ml) Chinese sweet soy sauce

1 tbsp (15 ml) oyster sauce

2 tbsp (30 ml) fish sauce

2 tsp (10 g) sugar

3 tbsp (45 ml) vegetable oil, divided

1 lb (450 g) chicken breast, sliced thin

2 cloves garlic, minced

2 eggs

1½ cups (335 g) broccoli florets

4 cups (960 g) fresh rice noodles, separated

½ tsp white pepper

Combine the Chinese sweet soy sauce, oyster sauce, fish sauce and sugar in a small bowl and set it aside.

Heat 2 tablespoons (30 ml) of oil on high in a large skillet for about 1 minute. When you see the first wisps of white smoke, add the chicken and garlic to the pan and sauté for about 1 minute or until the exterior of the chicken is mostly seared and opaque. Don't be scared to really scape the bits off the pan before they burn.

Add the remaining 1 tablespoon (15 ml) of oil to the pan and add in the eggs. Lightly scramble them until they are just set, about 30 seconds.

Add the broccoli, tossing it constantly until it starts to turn dark green, about 1 to 2 minutes.

Add the fresh rice noodles and allow them to sear in the pan and trade flavors with all the other ingredients for about 1 minute. Then add the sauce and stir constantly to combine for about 3 minutes until the noodles soak up the sauce and start to crisp slightly on the edges.

When the chicken is cooked through and the sauces are absorbed, sprinkle with white pepper and combine very well.

Pro Tip: To slightly precook the broccoli florets quickly, place them in a bowl with about 1 tablespoon (15 ml) of water. Microwave for 1½ minutes on high, remove, and you're ready to go. You've taken that raw taste and texture out of them to that perfect point to add them to the wok.

CLASSIC LO MEIN NOODLES

I love this deceptively simple dish. If you have all the ingredients, you can have a plate of delicious noodles on the table within 15 to

20 minutes, with prep included. There really isn't such a thing as a "lo mein" noodle, so don't try to find it on the shelf. You want to buy an egg noodle or pasta that's relatively thin and has some tooth. Some common names will be lo mein, chow mein, egg noodles or pancit noodles. Most markets have Japanese yaki soba noodles in the cold case, and those would work perfectly. Spaghetti or fettuccini cooked al dente and rinsed in cold water and drained in a colander will also make a great lo mein. The traditional difference between lo mein and chow mein is that lo mein is a soft noodle with some gravy, and chow mein is a crispy fried noodle tossed with or smothered in sauce. This has become very convoluted over the 200 years Chinese food has existed in America, with regional evolutions. Another tip: Although sesame oil is a fat and you would assume it should be used to start the stir-fry, I want you to treat it like a sauce. Sesame oil has incredible aroma and flavor but burns at a low temp. Add it to a sauce instead and use a high-temp oil like canola or peanut for cooking.

SERVES 4 TO 6

---

3 tbsp (45 ml) oyster sauce

1 tsp sesame oil

1 tbsp (15 ml) soy sauce

¼ cup (60 ml) chicken stock

1 tsp cornstarch

3 tbsp (45 ml) cooking oil

2 tsp (10 g) minced garlic

1½ tbsp (11 g) thinly sliced ginger

½ lb (250 g) chicken breast or thigh, thin sliced

3 cups (750 g) fresh lo mein noodles

¼ lb (125g) baby bok choy, bottoms removed

3 scallions, cut into 1½" (4-cm) pieces

To make the sauce, stir together the oyster sauce, sesame oil, soy sauce, chicken stock and cornstarch in a small bowl and reserve.

Heat the pan to high and add the oil. Once you see wisps of white smoke, add the garlic and ginger and cook until light brown and fragrant, about 20 seconds. Stir in the chicken and cook until medium, about 1 minute.

Stir in the noodles and bok choy and cook until the bok choy starts to soften and turn bright green, about 1 minute.

Stir in the sauce; allow the sauce to coat all the ingredients and start to simmer, about 1 more minute.

Cook until the chicken is cooked through (about 1 more minute) and sauce starts to bubble into a glaze. Top with scallions and serve hot.

SPICY GROUND PORK NOODLES (DAN DAN MIAN)

We all know that Italians learned how to make pasta from the Chinese. Long before there was Bolognese, there was dan dan noodles. The savory ground pork bathes the wheat noodles and pairs perfectly with the light spinach. In a pinch, you can use linguini noodles for this recipe and it will still be delicious. After all, we taught the Italians how to make them.

SERVES 4

Sauce

2 tbsp (14 g) thinly sliced ginger

¼ cup (60 ml) Chinese sweet soy sauce

¼ cup (60 ml) Chinese light soy sauce

1–2 tbsp (15–30 ml) sambal chili sauce

2 tsp (10 ml) Chinese black vinegar

½ tsp Sichuan peppercorn powder

Noodles

8 oz (500 g) Chinese dry wheat noodles

2 tbsp (30 ml) vegetable oil

2 tbsp (20 g) chopped garlic

4 tbsp (60 g) Tianjin preserved vegetable, rinsed

1 cup (225 g) baby spinach

1 lb (500 g) ground pork

3 tbsp (45 ml) sherry

3 scallions, green part only, thinly sliced

For the Sauce
Combine the sauce ingredients in a small bowl and reserve.

For the Noodles
Boil 3 quarts (2.8 L) of water in a 6-quart (5.7-L) pot. Cook the noodles for about 10 minutes or until al dente, rinse and drain well in a colander. Place the noodles in a large serving bowl.

Heat the vegetable oil in a wok over high heat. When you see wisps of white smoke, add the garlic, preserved vegetable and baby spinach to the wok and stir-fry for 30 seconds. Add the pork, breaking it up and tossing for 2 to 3 minutes, or until almost cooked through. Deglaze the pan with sherry and add the reserved sauce. Stir-fry, folding constantly, for 1 more minute or until pork is fully cooked.

Pour the meat sauce over the noodles and top with scallions.

> **Pro Tip:** Tianjin preserved vegetable is a salted cabbage similar to sauerkraut. It adds a delicious tang and umami. Leave it out if you can't find it. But it's available online and in many Asian stores.

JAPANESE NOODLE BOWL (NABEYAKI UDON—NOODLES IN POT)

Japanese noodle soups, to me, are the ultimate comfort food. This dish is a large bowl of udon noodles with a savory soy broth, veggies, shrimp and poached eggs. A large lidded earthenware bowl is called a nabe, hence the name Nabeyaki. Yaki translates to "cooked," so the title simply means "udon noodles cooked in a pot." It's an old authentic technique where you make your broth, add all items in the bowl uncooked, then let it all heat up together. This develops the flavors of all the ingredients with the broth.

SERVES 4

Noodle Broth (Kake-jiru)

4 cups (960 ml) Dashi Stock

2 tsp (10 g) salt

3 oz (90 ml) soy sauce

2 tbsp (30 g) sugar

2 tbsp (30 ml) mirin

Assembly

8 oz (228 g) dried udon noodles

¼ lb (95 g) medium shrimp, cleaned and deveined, tails left on

4 fresh shiitake mushrooms, sliced

2–3 scallions, sliced

1 egg

For the Broth

Combine all the broth ingredients in a small stockpot and bring them to a boil. Remove it from the heat and reserve it. The broth will keep for up to 3 to 5 days in the refrigerator.

To Assemble

To prepare the udon noodles, bring enough water to cover the noodles to a boil. Add the noodles and cook them until al dente, about 10 to 12 minutes. Shock them in cold water, rinse them and reserve.

In a donabe (Japanese casserole pot) or a medium saucepan, arrange the noodles on the bottom of the pot. Top the noodles with the shrimp, shiitake mushrooms and scallions. Ladle in enough stock to cover the noodles. Cover the pot and bring the contents to a simmer, about 6 minutes or until shrimp are pink. Crack an egg into the center of the pot, cover, and simmer about 4 minutes or until egg is cooked but soft in the middle. Serve as a one-pot meal.

COLD SOBA NOODLES WITH DIPPING SAUCE (ZARU SOBA)

Chilled buckwheat noodles (soba) are traditionally served on basketwork "plates" or in square bamboo boxes with slatted bottoms, accompanied by a cup (240 ml) of flavorful, cold dipping sauce. Strong wasabi horseradish and finely chopped green onion are mixed into the dipping sauce as desired. A perfect meal for a hot and humid summer day, this is a universal favorite, and every region has its own way of serving it.

SERVES 2 TO 4

½ lb soba (dried buckwheat noodles)

2½ cups (600 ml) Noodle Dipping Sauce

¼ cup (50 g) nori seaweed, finely shredded

4 tsp (20 g) wasabi horseradish

⅓ cup (16 g) finely chopped green onion

Bring 2 quarts (1.9 L) of water to boil in a 4-quart (3.8-L) pot. Boil dried soba noodles following package directions. Remove noodles, shock in cold running water, then rinse noodles with your hands to eliminate surface starch. Drain and divide among 4 plates.

Sprinkle nori shreds on each serving of noodles. Serve the dipping sauce in individual small bowls. Place spicy garnishes in serving dishes and let each diner help himself.

To eat like a pro, mix a dab of wasabi and about 1 tablespoon (20 g) of finely chopped green onion into the dipping sauce. Pick up the noodles, dip into the sauce and eat. It's OK to slurp.

NOODLE DIPPING SAUCE (TSUKE—JIRU)

This is the dipping sauce for the cold soba noodles. It's also great hot.

MAKES 3 CUPS (710 ML)

2 tsp (10 ml) instant dashi

2½ cups (600 ml) water

5 oz (150 ml) soy sauce

2 oz (60 ml) mirin

1 tsp sugar

3 cups (36 g) bonito flakes

In a medium-sized pot, mix all the ingredients except the bonito flakes and bring just to a boil over medium-high heat. Stir in the bonito flakes and immediately remove from the heat. Wait about 10 seconds, till the flakes are thoroughly soaked, and strain. Let the liquid cool to room temperature to use. You may prepare this dipping sauce in advance. It will keep several months refrigerated.

KOREAN CHAP CHAE (GLASS NOODLES WITH BEEF)

This delicious Korean pan-fried noodle dish is underappreciated and not well known. It's a great way to use the Bulgogi recipe (here). These noodles are made from potato starch, so they are like glass noodles—super slippery, low in carbs and loaded with deliciousness! You can sub just about any noodles that pan-fry well in this recipe, including spaghetti or linguini.

SERVES 4 TO 6

8 oz (240 g) cellophane wheat noodles (aka potato starch noodles)

2–4 tbsp (30–60 ml) cooking oil

2 cloves garlic, chopped

8 oz (240 g) Bulgogi

10 mushrooms, quartered

½ medium onion, chopped

½ carrot, julienned

½ green bell pepper, julienned

1 cup (30 g) baby spinach

1 tbsp (8 g) sesame seeds, toasted

2 tbsp (30 ml) sesame oil

½ cup (120 ml) soy sauce

2 tbsp (30 g) sugar

Salt and pepper to taste

Bring 3 quarts (2.8 L) of water to a rolling boil in a 6-quart (5.7-L) stockpot. Boil the noodles for about 6 to 8 minutes, until al dente.

Drain into a colander and run under cold water for a few minutes to cool down and rinse the starch off. Drain them thoroughly, then cut the noodles to 3- or 4-inch (7.6- or 10-cm) lengths and reserve them.

Heat oil in a large skillet over high heat for about 1 to 2 minutes. Add the garlic, stirring constantly for about 30 seconds. Add the Bulgogi to the pan and cook until medium doneness, about 2 to 3 minutes. Add the mushrooms, onion, carrot and green pepper and cook until slightly tender, about 1 minute. Add the noodles and spinach and keep it all moving to combine. Stir in the sesame seeds, sesame oil, soy sauce, sugar, pepper and salt. Cook for an additional minute until the noodles are coated well in the sauce and all the vegetables soften a little.

VEGAN DRUNKEN NOODLES

I've been serving this version in my restaurants for years, and it's great for meatless Mondays. Vegetarian oyster sauce can be found all over the interweb and is the key to making this vegan version. Maggi sauce is a soy sauce product that is enhanced with other seasonings and full of umami.

SERVES 2 TO 4

Sauce

5 tbsp (75 ml) sweet soy sauce

3 tbsp (45 ml) vegetarian oyster sauce

3 tbsp (45 ml) Maggi sauce

2 tbsp (30 g) sugar

2 tsp (10 ml) sriracha sauce

2 tsp (6 g) minced garlic

6–8 Thai basil leaves, chiffonade cut

Drunken Noodles

3 tbsp (45 ml) canola or peanut oil

2– 3 cloves garlic, minced

1–2 serrano chilies, sliced thin

5 oz (145 g) extra-firm tofu, cut into ¾" (2-cm) large dice

½ medium white onion, sliced

3– 4 cups (675–910 g) fresh rice noodles, separated

½ cup (120 g) grape tomatoes, halved

1 cup (40 g) Thai basil leaves, loosely packed

For the Sauce

Combine the sauce ingredients in a small bowl and set it aside.

For the Drunken Noodles

Heat the oil over medium-high heat in a medium-sized sauté pan. At the first wisps of white smoke, sauté the garlic until it is light brown. Stir in the chilies, diced tofu and onion, folding constantly until the tofu starts to brown, about 1 to 2 minutes.

Add the fresh rice noodles and sauté until the noodles are soft and slightly browned on the edges, about 2 minutes.

Add the sauce, tomatoes and basil. Toss them together to combine for about 3 to 5 minutes. Make sure the noodles completely absorb the sauce.

VEGAN PAD THAI

Vegan food is delicious! Yeah, I said it, and I'll prove it to you. Most run from the V word, and it's really because most chefs don't know how to cook without meat. The simple fact is meat and meat products are naturally full of umami, so anyone can make them delicious. Making vegetables, fruits and starches tasty is harder but totally doable. It's about retraining your brain to think about flavors. Learning new sauce and flavor combinations is key. For this dish, we're replacing fish sauce with soy or amino acid sauce and leaving out the dried shrimp. Check out amino acid sauces if you are cooking more vegan. Sounds like a science experiment, but they are a great sub for fish sauce and good for Asian dishes.

SERVES 4

3 cups (720 g) pad Thai noodles (rice stick)

3 tbsp (45 ml) soy sauce or Bragg Liquid Aminos

1 tbsp (15 g) Thai tamarind paste

1 tsp rice vinegar

4 tbsp (50 g) sugar

¼ cup (60 ml) water

2 tbsp (30 ml) oil

3–4 cloves garlic, rough chopped

½ cup (95 g) diced baked tofu

1½ tbsp (23 g) minced packaged sweet pickled turnip

1 tbsp (8 g) paprika (optional)

3–4 green onions, cut into 2" (5-cm) pieces on the bias

¼ cup (50 g) chopped unsalted dry-roasted peanuts, divided

1 cup (40 g) bean sprouts

Soak the dry noodles in a large bowl of warm (90°F [32°C]) water for about an hour. The noodles will start to absorb water, loosen up and be ready for the pan. If using fresh noodles, you can just open the package and add to the pan at the appropriate time.

To make the sauce, combine the soy sauce, tamarind paste, rice vinegar, sugar and water in a small bowl. Make sure to stir well until the sugar dissolves.

Heat a skillet or wok over high heat for about 1 minute or until the pan gets pretty hot. Add oil and swirl to coat the pan completely. When the pan just starts to smoke, add the garlic and stir about 5 seconds. Add the tofu and turnip, stir-fry until they begin to get fragrant, about 1 minute.

Add the drained noodles and cook for about 2 to 3 minutes, until soft. Add the reserved sauce mixture and paprika and fold together until paprika evenly colors the noodles and all the liquid is absorbed, about 2 minutes.

Place the green onions in the center of the noodles, and then spoon some noodles over the green onions to cover and let steam 30 seconds. Stir in 3 tablespoons (30 g) peanuts. Transfer to the serving plate and garnish with the bean sprouts and remaining peanuts.

SOUPS, CURRIES AND LARGER PLATES

The term "large plate" is pretty relative in the Asian culinary universe but still very important. Like the flavor balance in the yum, there should be an ingredient balance as well. It would be rare to eat multiple courses of the same type of meat or starch. You would rarely see two different rice dishes or multiple noodle dishes on a table. What you would eat at every meal are combinations of foods. For example, you would have a vegetable, a land animal, seafood and a starch to round out the table.

In this chapter, you're going to find some great classics, like Tom Yum Soup, Miso Soup and Wonton Soup). I hope you discover some new greats, like Steamed Fish with Ginger and Scallion. Make something familiar, then branch out with something totally new.

Cooking techniques are also separated by method. The first way to break down cooking is two worlds of moist and dry heat. Moist methods will be boiling, steaming, braising etc. Dry would be sautéing, roasting, baking, grilling and frying (believe it or not). Most of these dishes in this section utilize the moist heat method.

Curry is kind of funny because it uses a combination of methods. You start out by frying the curry paste (dry heat) but then add coconut milk to braise items in the wok or pan. The history and techniques are in the pages ahead, but one very important method to remember when using coconut milk is to never shake the can. I know what you're thinking—even the damn can says to shake the can. But a real Asian cook knows there are actually three ingredients in a can of coconut milk. Undisturbed, the top 13% to 19% of the can is pure coconut oil, great for sautéing. The lower part is light coconut milk. Shaken together, it's a fuller fat coconut milk. Each has its use, and Thai curry is a great way to utilize all three.

PANANG CHICKEN CURRY

The word curry or kare simply means a spiced sauce, not too
different from a gumbo or mole. Thais usually use coconut milk as

the liquid, and we use fresh herbs as the flavor base. To make a base curry paste, grind together lemongrass, shallots, kaffir lime leaves, garlic and shrimp paste to form a smooth paste. If you finish that paste with red chilies, you make red curry paste. Green chilies make green curry. Panang is made with a combination of red chilies and dried chilies and goes great with chicken, beef or duck.

SERVES 4 TO 6

---

6 cups (1.4 L) full-fat coconut milk, with 3 tbsp (45 ml) of the cream separated out

4 tbsp (60 g) panang curry paste

2 kaffir lime leaves, cut into a fine chiffonade

½ cup (95 g) thinly sliced brown onion

½ cup (95 g) roughly chopped, whole with stems, Thai sweet basil

1½ lb (680 g) chicken breast, sliced into ¼"- (6-mm)-thick tiles

1 cup (240 g) canned sliced bamboo shoots

½ cup (95 g) sliced red bell pepper

2 tsp (10 ml) fish sauce

½ tbsp (10 g) tamarind paste

1 tsp sugar

In a medium saucepan, heat the 3 tablespoons (45 ml) of the thick coconut cream on high for about 1 minute. When the cream starts to sizzle, stir the curry paste into the cream like building a roux. Add the lime leaves. Stir-fry the paste for about 1 minute, until the paste starts to thicken, dry out and become fragrant. If the curry starts to sputter, add a small amount of coconut milk to keep the paste moving. Cook the paste until it has the consistency of peanut butter.

Stir the onion, basil and remaining coconut milk into the curry paste. Heat until you reach a full rolling boil. Allow the curry to boil for about 10 to 20 minutes or until it reduces by about one-fourth or coats the back of a wooden spoon.

Reduce the heat to a simmer. Add the chicken, bamboo shoots, red bell pepper, fish sauce, tamarind and sugar. Let this simmer for about 10 minutes, or until the chicken is cooked through. Serve hot over cooked rice.

Pro Tip: Don't forget: never, ever shake the can of coconut milk! You want the cream to naturally separate and rise to top. You can use that natural coconut cream like cooking oil to fry your curry pastes!

THAI GREEN CURRY WITH CHICKEN AND SWEET POTATO

You can apply this recipe to any type of curry you like. If you like your food really spicy, try adding dried chili flakes or whole fresh chilies. Curry is a simple, hearty dish; get as creative as you want! As always, practice makes perfect.

SERVES 4

6 cups (1.4 L) full-fat coconut milk, with 3 tbsp (45 ml) of the cream separated out

4–6 tbsp (60–90 g) green curry paste

1½ (700 g) sweet potatoes, peeled and cut into 1″ (2.5-cm) dice

½ small brown onion, thinly sliced

½ cup (20 g) roughly chopped, whole with stems, Thai sweet basil

1½ lb (700 g) chicken thighs, sliced into bite-size pieces

½ red bell pepper, cut into small dice

2 tsp fish sauce

1 tbsp (15 ml) tamarind paste

1 tsp sugar

2 kaffir lime leaves, sliced very thin

In a medium saucepan, heat the 3 tablespoons (45 ml) of the thick coconut cream on high for about 1 minute. When the cream starts to sizzle, stir the curry paste into the cream like building a roux. Stir-fry the paste for about 1 minute, until the paste starts to thicken, dry out and become fragrant. If the curry starts to sputter, add a small amount of coconut milk to keep the paste moving. Cook the paste until it has the consistency of peanut butter.

Stir in the sweet potato cubes, onion, basil and remaining coconut milk into the curry paste. Increase the heat to high until you reach a full rolling boil, then reduce to a simmer. Let the curry simmer for about 10 to 15 minutes or until the potatoes are fork-tender. Also check that the curry is thick enough to coat the back of a wooden spoon.

Add the chicken and bell pepper, fish sauce, tamarind and sugar. Let this simmer for about 5 more minutes, or until the chicken is cooked through. Serve hot over cooked rice. Garnish with the Thai basil and kaffir lime leaves.

HOT AND SOUR EGG DROP SOUP

Another comfort classic that is fast and easy to put together. You can play around with the vegetable combinations according to your preferences. Make sure not to whip the eggs too quickly; you want to create large fluffy sheets of egg instead of tiny laces of eggs. The "hot" in this soup is often confused with "spicy"; if you want spicy, add 1 tablespoon (10 g) of dried chili flakes to this recipe.

SERVES 4

4 cups (960 ml) Chinese Chicken Stock

4 fresh shiitake mushrooms, sliced thin

⅓ cup (85 g) bamboo shoots, diced

1 tsp soy sauce

½ tsp white sugar

1 tsp salt

½ tsp ground white pepper

2 tbsp (30 ml) red wine vinegar

1 tsp sesame oil

2 tbsp (15 g) cornstarch

2 tbsp (30 ml) water

½ (16-oz [240-g]) package firm tofu, cubed

1 egg

2 tbsp (6 g) thinly sliced green onions

Heat chicken stock over medium-high heat in a medium saucepan until simmering.

Stir in the mushroom and bamboo shoots, soy sauce, sugar, salt, white pepper, vinegar and sesame oil and let simmer for about 5 minutes. You can adjust the flavors according to your preference here.

In a separate small bowl, combine the cornstarch with 2 tablespoons (30 ml) of water to make a slurry. Pour the slurry into the soup while constantly stirring. It will start to thicken as the soup bubbles and simmers. Add the tofu, and cook for an additional minute. Crack the egg into a bowl and whisk until the white and yolk are an even yellow. Drizzle the raw egg into the simmering soup; turn off the heat. Stir in a figure-eight pattern until you see the egg ribbons start to form. Serve hot and garnish with green onions.

TOM YUM SOUP

The most popular Thai soup, Tom Yum Soup is known for its
medicinal and restorative properties (some say it's a close rival to

chicken noodle!). I prefer to serve the dish with the whole pieces of galangal, lemongrass and kaffir lime leaves from the stock, but feel free to strain them out if the pieces are too big or their flavors are too strong.

MAKES 1 QUART (946 ML)

---

4 cups (960 ml) Thai Chicken Stock

8–10 medium shrimp, peeled and deveined

1 (15-oz [425-g]) can whole peeled straw mushrooms, drained and rinsed

2–4 dried Thai chilies or chiles de arbol, depending on desired heat level

4–6 tbsp (60–90 ml) fish sauce

1 tsp granulated chicken bouillon

6 tbsp (60–90 ml) lime juice

3 tbsp (45 g) chili paste in soybean oil

3 kaffir lime leaves

Cilantro sprigs to garnish

Bring the Thai Chicken Stock to a simmer over medium-high heat in a 3-quart (2.8-L) saucepan. Once the broth is simmering, add the shrimp, mushrooms and chilies and cook for about 2 to 3 minutes or until the shrimp are pink and almost cooked through.

Stir in the fish sauce, the bouillon, the lime juice and the chili paste. The chili paste is thick like honey and might need some help to break apart and incorporate into the soup. A whisk works great for this.

Taste and adjust the soup. For more salt, add fish sauce. If you are lacking acid, add more lime juice. Garnish with lime leaves and cilantro.

COCONUT CHICKEN SOUP (TOM KHA GAI)

Kha is the Thai word for galangal, an herb that resembles ginger but tastes nothing like it. It's very spicy and herbaceous, with a strong pine scent. It's refreshing and the backbone of this delicious soup. There's much debate about chicken breast versus thigh. I personally love chicken thighs, and they would work in any of my recipes. Feel free to play around with your ratios of coconut milk to stock. If you want a creamier soup, up the coconut milk.

MAKES 1 QUART (946 ML)

3 cups (720 ml) Thai Chicken Stock

6 oz (180 g) boneless, skinless chicken breasts, cut into 1" (2.5-cm) cubes

1 (15-oz [425-g]) can straw mushrooms, drained

1–3 Thai chilies, split

5 tbsp (75 ml) fish sauce

4 tbsp (60 ml) lime juice

1 (14-oz [414-ml]) can coconut milk (not light)

1 tbsp (15 ml) chili paste in soybean oil

1½ cups (330 g) chopped cabbage

Kaffir (Thai) lime leaves, for garnish

Cilantro leaves, for garnish

Bring the Thai Chicken Stock to a simmer over medium-high heat in a large pot.

Add the chicken, mushrooms and chilies and cook until the chicken is cooked through, about 4 minutes.

Stir in the fish sauce, lime juice, coconut milk and chili paste. Add the chopped cabbage and cook until just tender, about 1 minute.

Divide the soup among serving bowls and garnish each with 1 to 2 lime leaves and cilantro.

Pro Tip: Chili paste with soybean oil is uniquely Thai. The name might lead you to think it's spicy, but it's very mild. It adds a lot of umami notes and its beautiful signature red hue.

RED MISO SOUP WITH TOFU

Miso paste is pure umami. One of the most complex combinations of savory, salty and naturally sweet, it has only three ingredients. It

comes in three levels of fermentation, aka intensity. White miso is sweeter, less savory. Yellow is in the middle, with a balanced savory sweetness. It is also the most common and most used miso. Red is fermented longer and has a pleasantly intense flavor. I prefer it, and I think you will love it. Dashi stock is one of the fundamental building blocks of Japanese cuisine and is best when made from scratch (see here). The marriage of dashi and miso in miso soup is a beautiful combination. The salt is controlled by the amount of miso. If you like your soup a little saltier and more robust, add more miso as desired.

SERVES 4

3–4 cups (710–946 ml) Dashi Stock

¼ cup (50 g) fresh shiitake mushrooms, sliced very thin

¼ cup (50g) dried wakame seaweed, rinsed and chopped

¼–½ cup (50–100 g) red miso

4 oz (100 g) block soft tofu in water, cut into small cubes

2–3 scallions, finely sliced on a bias

Heat the stock in a medium saucepan over medium heat until just under a simmer.

Add the mushrooms and seaweed and allow to cook for about 5 minutes or until the mushrooms have softened.

Submerge a small sieve into the saucepan until the rim is just above the stock. Add the miso into the sieve and use a wooden spoon to work the miso through into the soup. This will prevent lumps from forming. Stir well and taste the soup; if not salty enough, add additional miso.

Add the tofu and scallions; allow to cook for about a minute. The scallions will perfume the soup and give it an earthy sweetness.

WONTON SOUP

Wontons are technically dumplings, very similar in fact to a sew mai. The two fillings are totally interchangeable. The little soup dumplings are also delicious by themselves without the broth. You can boil them up and serve them on a plate, slathered with some chili or soy for a great appetizer.

MAKES 24 WONTONS

Filling

1 lb (450 g) lean pork, coarsely ground

1 lb (450 g) shrimp, coarsely chopped

2 tbsp (30 ml) thin soy sauce

2 tbsp (30 ml) oyster sauce

Few drops sesame oil

2 tsp (10 ml) sherry

1 tsp sugar

1 green onion, minced

1 tsp cornstarch

Pinch salt

2 dashes white pepper

Soup

24 wonton wrappers

3 qt (2.8 L) water for boiling wontons

5 cups (1.2 L) Chinese Chicken Stock

3 scallions, thinly sliced

1 tsp sesame oil

For the Filling

Combine all the filling ingredients in a large bowl, mixing them together well. Lay one wonton wrapper in front of you. Cover the remaining wonton wrappers with a damp towel to keep them from drying out. Moisten all the edges of the wonton wrapper with water. Place a heaping teaspoon of filling in the center.

For the Soup

Fold the wonton wrapper in half lengthwise, making sure the ends meet. Press down firmly on the ends to seal the wonton. Use your thumbs to push down on the edges of the filling to center it. Keeping your thumbs in place, fold over the wonton wrapper one more time. Push the corners up and hold it in place between your thumb and index finger. Wet the corners with your fingers and bring the two ends together so that they overlap. Press them to seal. The finished product should resemble tortellini. Repeat with the remaining wontons.

Bring the water to a boil in a large pot. Add the wontons, making sure there is enough room for them to move about freely. Let the wontons boil for 5 to 8 minutes, until they rise to the top and the filling is cooked through. Remove them from the pot with a slotted spoon.

Bring the Chinese Chicken Stock to a boil in a large pot. Add the wontons and bring the soup back to a boil. Add the green onion, remove the pot from the heat and add the sesame oil, stirring. Ladle into soup bowls, allowing 3 to 4 wontons per person.

DEEP—FRIED TROUT WITH GREEN MANGO SLAW

I love fried fresh fish. It's crispy, moist and reminds me of being on the Mekong River in Thailand. I've adapted this dish for an easy-to-find market fish. Trout is great fried because it's not too dense and has all the crispy bits I love from the skin to the eyeballs. But if you like a tamer fried fillet, that's fine too. The juxtaposition of the dry, savory, crispy fish paired with the refreshing sweet-and-sour salad is delicious. I made this dish during my Iron Chef battle with Morimoto and nearly beat him with it.

SERVES 4 TO 6

2 lb (900 g) trout fillets, scaled

Salt and pepper

2 shallots, finely sliced

1 clove garlic, finely chopped

1–3 Thai chilies, sliced thin

½ cup (120 ml) lime juice

½ cup (120 ml) fish sauce

½ cup (95 g) brown sugar or palm sugar

2 cups (450 g) matchstick-cut green mango (green apples are a great sub)

½ red onion, thinly sliced

¼–½ cup (50–95 g) cashew nuts, roasted

1½ qt (1.4 L) oil for frying

3 eggs

2 cups (250 g) flour for dredging

2 cups (100 g) panko breadcrumbs

Cut the trout filets in half and season lightly with salt and pepper. Thoroughly pat them dry with paper towels and set aside.

In a small saucepan, combine the shallots, garlic and Thai chilies over low heat. Stir in the lime juice, fish sauce and sugar. Let the mixture heat up to right below a simmer. Stir it until the sugar dissolves, then remove it from the heat. Transfer the mixture to a bowl and chill it until ready to serve. When you're ready to serve the fish, add the mango, red onion and nuts.

Heat the oil in a 4- to 5-quart (3.8- to 4.7-L) Dutch oven or pot until the oil reaches 360°F (182°C). In a medium bowl, crack the eggs and whisk until even. In another bowl, add the flour. Place the panko breadcrumbs in a third bowl. Congrats, you've just created a breading station. Dredge the fish in flour and shake off the excess. Dip the fish in egg, then immediately roll it in panko. Knock off any excess and gently place into the fryer. Fry the fish for about 5 minutes on each side, until cooked through. Drain it on paper towels then serve immediately with the slaw.

STEAMED SNAPPER FILLET WITH GINGER AND SCALLION

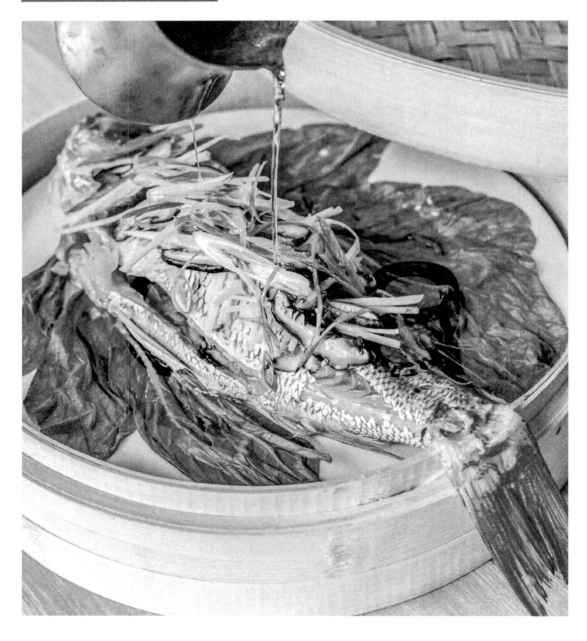

This is a classic Cantonese dish that my grandmother made for us weekly. The savory soy sauce is the secret here; it adds so much umami to this dish. And drizzling the hot oil over scallions releases a lot of aroma and is a cool technique to impress your friends with. If you don't like your food staring back at you, you can always use filets here. Halibut is a pretty easy fish to find and works great. Stay with the white-meat fish and you will be great!

SERVES 4

Sauce

1 tbsp (15 ml) shao shing rice cooking wine

3 tbsp (45 ml) light soy sauce

4 tbsp (60 ml) water

1 tbsp (8 g) chicken bouillon powder

1 tsp sesame oil

2 tsp (10 g) sugar

Snapper

2 lb (900 g) small rockfish, like snapper, scaled with skin on

Pinch salt

Pinch white pepper

4 Chinese black mushrooms, soaked in warm water until soft, then sliced thin

4 baby bok choy, quartered

2" (5-cm) piece ginger, finely sliced like grass

2 tbsp (30 ml) sesame oil

2 tbsp (30 ml) canola oil

3 scallions, finely sliced like grass

For the Sauce

Mix all the sauce ingredients in a small sauce pan. Bring the sauce to a simmer; stir until the solids have dissolved. Remove from heat and reserve.

For the Snapper

Rinse the fish with cold water and pat it dry with paper towels. Season it with salt and pepper.

Place the fish skin-side up in a heatproof dish. Evenly sprinkle the mushrooms and ginger over the top. Lay the baby bok choy pieces around the fish like a frame.

Steam the fish on high for about 10 to 15 minutes or until it's cooked through. The fish should flake apart easily. Carefully discard any excess liquid from the dish and place the scallions on top.

Combine the oils in a small saucepan and heat them to high for about 2 minutes or until just smoking. Drizzle the hot oil over the scallions; they will crackle. Finish by spooning the sauce over the fish.

INDIAN DAL (YELLOW LENTILS)

I love dishes that have multiple uses. Dal is just the Indian word for "legumes." This dish uses yellow lentils to make a hearty savory stew. But wait, there's more! If you thin it out with more stock, it makes the perfect lentil soup. It's also important to learn the importance of blooming spices. Blooming is the waking up of spices with hot oil. Like you would sauté onions and garlic to open up their flavors, the same applies to spices.

SERVES 4

2 tbsp (30 ml) vegetable oil

1 medium onion, finely chopped

2 cloves garlic, minced

2 serrano chilies, sliced (leave out if you don't want any heat)

2 tsp (10 g) kosher salt

½ tsp turmeric powder

½ tsp garam masala

½ tsp coriander powder

½ tsp cumin powder

2 cups (500 g) yellow dal lentils, rinsed and picked through

3 cups (750 ml) water or chicken stock

1 (14.5-oz [411-g]) can chopped tomatoes

2 tbsp (28 g) butter

¼ cup (10 g) roughly chopped cilantro

Heat a 2-quart (1.9-L) saucepan to high and add the oil. After about 1 minute, stir in the onion, garlic, chilies and salt. Sauté for about a minute, until the onion starts to become translucent. Stir in all the spices and keep them moving for about 30 seconds. This will bloom them—but be careful not to burn them.

Place the rinsed lentils into the pan and cover with water or chicken stock. Pour in the can of chopped tomatoes. Give it all a good stir to make sure nothing is stuck to the bottom. Reduce your heat until you achieve a low consistent simmer. Cover, leaving the lid just slightly cracked to allow some evaporation and keep it from boiling over. Cook for about 45 minutes, stirring every 10 minutes, scraping the bottom. It should look like a thick chowder, so add water as needed. Once the lentils are creamy and soft, finish by swirling in butter and cilantro.

BRAISED VEGETABLE KORMA

This is a great vegetarian curry. It eats like a creamy vegetable stew, perfect served over a bowl of basmati rice. Paneer is a fresh Indian cheese very similar to Mexican queso fresco. You can sub queso fresco or a firm fresh mozzarella. No matter what cheese you go with, brown it in a very hot pan with some oil to keep its texture.

SERVES 4

2 tbsp (30 ml) vegetable oil

1 medium onion, small dice

½ tsp minced garlic

½ tsp minced ginger

1 tsp cayenne pepper

½ tsp turmeric powder

1 tsp coriander powder

1 tsp Garam masala

1 (8-oz [240-ml]) can tomato sauce

1 cup (240 ml) water

½ cup (95 g) sliced carrots, cut into bias coins

½ cup (95 g) diced green bell pepper

½ cup (95 g) green beans, cut into 1" (2.5-cm) pieces

½ cup (75 g) peas

1 cup (240 g) diced waxy potatoes

4 oz (95 g) paneer, cubed and browned in a separate pan and reserved

¼ cup (60 ml) milk

¼ cup (60 ml) heavy cream

⅓ cup (85 g) cashews, roasted

Salt to taste

Heat the oil in a 4-quart (3.8-L) saucepan over medium-high heat for about 1 minute. Stir the onion into the skillet and cook it until it's translucent, about 2 minutes. Mix in the garlic and ginger, and cook them for 1 minute until fragrant.

Stir in the cayenne pepper, turmeric, coriander and Garam masala and cook them until they bubble slightly to bloom them. Stir in the tomato sauce and water, incorporating them well. Add the carrots, green bell pepper, beans, peas, potatoes and browned paneer. Bring it to a boil. Reduce the heat to low, and simmer it for 20 minutes, until the potatoes are tender.

Stir the milk, cream, and cashews into the skillet with the vegetables. Bring them to a boil, and continue cooking them for 2 to 3 minutes. Add salt to taste and serve.

SUSHI, SALADS AND OTHER VEGGIES

If you were attending French culinary school, as I did so many years ago, these dishes would in your garde-manger rotation. The French

brigade system classifies foods by not just cooking method but also by temperature. Garde-manger translates to the "keeper of the food," technically the keeper of the cold or refrigerated food. Back in the day, there wasn't refrigeration, so he or she stayed in the cool part of the kitchen. Garde-manger also produces the beautiful finger foods like canapes, salads and charcuterie, and did the fruit and ice carvings. So it made sense to put sushi in this chapter.

Sushi is really all about the rice, because fish is so consistent in terms of the availability and quality. But the true test of the sushi master is the rice, and you'll be learning how to make great rice.

I've put all the wonderful salads and cold veggies here from the very traditional Thai Papaya Salad to the new but necessary Chinese Chicken Salad. I think you'll find that Asian salads are dressed very differently. There are no oils added to make emulsions; they therefore eat lighter and have a lot of flavor.

CALIFORNIA ROLL

I think this should be called the LA Roll or the LA California roll because that's exactly where it was created, in a restaurant called

Tokyo Kaikan. I used to eat there all the time with my mom in the 1970s and 1980s. Some will say it was created in Canada, but I totally disagree. California rolls taste better with real crab, and that's how they were created. Lump crab and snow crab legs are great and easy to find. If you opt for the imitation stuff, I won't judge you … much. I think this dish is as authentic as any other Asian dish that has been created by and consumed by Asians. Tempura was created for the Portuguese fishermen who didn't want to eat raw fish. Does that take away from the authenticity? No way.

MAKES 8 ROLLS

---

1 lb (450 g) crab or surimi (imitation crab)

2 tbsp (15 g) mayonnaise (optional)

8 nori half sheets

6 cups (1.5 kg) Sushi Rice

2½ tbsp (50 g) prepared wasabi paste

1 hothouse cucumber, cut into 4″ (10-cm) batonnets

1 avocado, sliced into strips

2 tbsp (15 g) sesame seeds

Wasabi and pickled ginger, to garnish

Soy sauce, for dipping

In a small bowl, fold together the crab and mayonnaise until well combined, reserve.

Use a small bowl of water with 1 tablespoon (15 ml) of rice vinegar to keep your hands moist. This will keep rice from sticking to your hands. Lay a bamboo sushi-rolling mat down on a cutting board with the long side lined up close to your body. Place one sheet of nori rough-side up with the long side lined up with the edge of the mat.

Grab about ¾ cup (190 g, about a loose tennis ball of rice) and spread the rice into a thin, even layer across the whole nori sheet, leaving an uncovered ½-inch (1.3-cm) strip at the top. Rub 1 teaspoon of wasabi lengthwise down the middle. Right over that smear, place 3 tablespoons (100 g) of crab, 1 strip of cucumber and a strip of avocado. Sprinkle with 1 teaspoon of sesame seeds. Don't overstuff.

Lift up the back edge of the mat and use the tips of your fingers to contain the filling and rice as you roll. Continue rolling the sushi by pulling forward on the folded-over edge of the bamboo mat, rolling over a little at a time until rolled over. Once the roll is sealed, place the roll on the board and snug it down with the mat.

Moisten the edge of a sharp knife, slice the roll in half. Line up the two halves. Wipe your blade down with a damp towel and cut the two half rolls into three equal pieces. Repeat for the remaining 7 rolls. Serve with extra wasabi, pickled ginger and soy sauce.

> **Pro Tip:** I'm not a fan of having too many tools, but a bamboo mat is necessary. Nice thing is, they're cheap, and you can get them from the interweb. Wrap them in plastic to keep rice from sticking and prolong their lives.

SPICY TUNA ROLL

We all love spicy tuna for its spicy, creamy and fresh taste. I think it's so versatile, perfect to load into sushi rolls or a topping for salads or rice bowls too. Sushi-grade fish means a lot of things. It's usually caught, filleted and frozen right on the boat to maintain maximum freshness. Not all beautiful tuna in the fish case is sushi-grade, and you can get very sick from eating raw fish that isn't. So make sure you are buying from a reputable source. And not all tuna is the same. Make sure you are using at least yellowfin, but my favorite choice for spicy tuna would be bigeye. You can also play with the amount of sriracha depending on your desired heat levels.

MAKES 8 ROLLS

---

1 lb (450 g) sushi-grade raw tuna, cut into large dice

4 tbsp (60 g) mayonnaise

2–4 tbsp (30–60 g) Sriracha, depending on desired heat level

1 tbsp (15 ml) rice wine vinegar

8 nori half sheets

6 cups (1.5 kg) Sushi Rice

2½ tbsp (5 g) prepared wasabi paste

1 hothouse cucumber, cut into 4″ (10-cm) batonnets

1 tbsp (8 g) sesame seeds

Wasabi and pickled ginger, to garnish

Soy sauce, for dipping

Place the tuna, mayo and Sriracha in a clean food processor. Pulse until the Sriracha and mayo are uniformly mixed into the tuna but the tuna is still chunky.

Use a small bowl of water with the rice vinegar to keep your hands moist. This will keep the rice from sticking to your hands. Lay a bamboo sushi-rolling mat down on a cutting board with the long side lined up close to your body. Place one sheet of nori rough-side up with the long side lined up with the edge of the mat.

Grab about ¾ cup (190 g, about a loose tennis ball) of rice and spread it into a thin, even layer across the whole nori sheet, leaving an uncovered ½-inch (1.3-cm) strip at the top. Spread 1 teaspoon of wasabi lengthwise down the middle. Right over that smear, place 3 tablespoons (25 g) of spicy tuna and a strip of cucumber, and sprinkle with 1 teaspoon of sesame seeds. Don't overstuff.

Lift up the back edge of the mat and use the tips of your fingers to contain the filling and rice as you roll. Continue rolling the sushi by pulling forward on the folded-over edge of the bamboo mat, rolling over a little at a time until rolled over. Once the roll is sealed, place the roll on the board and snug it down with the mat.

Moisten the edge of a sharp knife and slice the roll in half. Line up the two halves. Wipe your blade down with a damp towel and cut the two half rolls into three equal pieces. Serve with extra wasabi, pickled ginger and soy sauce.

CUCUMBER KIMCHI (OI SOBAGI)

This is an easy kimchi recipe to make. Cucumbers ferment the quickest, about 1 day out of the fridge. Use this recipe and method to make any kimchi you like—Napa cabbage is the most common. Remember to ferment other items like cabbage for longer. You can play around with fermentation time and temp until you get the perfect sour funky balance you like.

MAKES 3 QUARTS (2.8 L)

½ gallon plus ⅓ cup (1.9 L plus 80 ml) water

¾ cup plus 1 tbsp (196 g) salt, divided

20 Persian or Japanese cucumbers

10 cloves garlic, minced

1 onion, cut into ½" (13-mm) dice

1 bunch green onions, sliced into ½" (13-mm) lengths

1 bunch garlic chives (buchu), cut into ½" (13-mm) pieces

½ cup (95 g) Korean ground chili

1 tsp sugar, plus 1 tsp as optional

Mix ½ gallon (1.9 L) of water with ¾ cup (180 g) of salt, stirring until the salt dissolves, to make a brine.

Soak the cucumbers in salt water for 30 minutes, no longer.

Remove the cucumbers from the brine and rinse. Cut about ¼ of an inch (6-mm) from each end of the cucumbers. Cut the cucumbers in half in the middle, not lengthwise. Hold the cucumber facing the circular middle. Cut them in half lengthwise, leaving about ½ inch (⅓ cm) at the end uncut. Cut them in half lengthwise again, perpendicular to your first cut, leaving the end uncut. You should have 4 semi-equal parts of cucumber, cut but still attached. Repeat with the remaining cucumbers.

Combine the onion, green onions, buchu, ground chili, 1 tablespoon (16 g) of salt, and 1 teaspoon optional sugar in a large bowl. I recommend wearing gloves for this.

Set 3 (1-quart [946-ml]) jars on your work surface. Using your fingers, separate the cucumber quarters and stuff the mix into the cucumbers. Divide them evenly among the jars, pressing the cucumbers down firmly into the jars.

Stir 1 teaspoon of sugar into ⅓ cup (80 ml) of water until the sugar is completely dissolved. Pour the sugar water over the cucumbers.

Let it sit 1 day before serving. Cucumber Kimchi ferments very quickly. Refrigerate it after opening.

PAPAYA SALAD (SOM TUM)

Thailand borrowed this dish from Laos and made it a little more palate friendly. It has a clean, crisp, refreshing quality but perfectly captures the spirit of huge flavors of the yum. Green papayas are readily available at Asian and Latin markets. They are the same long papayas eaten ripe, just picked green and young. If they are tough to find, you can sub in a julienned fruit or vegetable blend including carrots, apples and cabbage. All work great for this recipe. Thai salted shrimp are little orange baby-sized shrimp that have been salted and dried. They add amazing umami (savory) and salt to this and any dish.

SERVES 4

Dressing
¼ cup (60 ml) fish sauce

¼ cup (60 ml) lime juice

¼ cup (50 g) palm or brown sugar

2 cloves garlic, minced

1 tbsp (15 g) dried salted shrimp

1–3 Thai chiles, minced

Salad
4 cups (1.9 kg) young green papaya, grated

1 cup (240 g) long beans, cut on the bias into 1½" (4-cm) lengths, divided

8–10 cherry tomatoes, quartered, divided

1 cup (240 g) chopped roasted peanuts

For the Dressing
Place the dressing ingredients, 4 tomatoes and a quarter of the long beans into a blender and pulse them together for about 5 seconds. The dressing should be slightly chunky. The amount of chilies used depends on how spicy you like your food.

For the Papaya Salad

In a large bowl, toss the papaya, remaining long beans, remaining tomatoes and some of the peanuts together with the dressing to taste. Make sure to aggressively mix the ingredients to slightly break up the tomatoes and beans. Garnish the salad with the remaining peanuts.

CHICKEN LARB—THAI MINCED CHICKEN SALAD

This tangier version of the chicken salad is influenced by the "Isaarn," or northeastern, area of Thailand. The northern version is more savory, with a variety of pork offal meats like liver and cracklings. Northern food is very healthy and delicious. Always serve with a variety of fresh vegetable crudités.

SERVES 4 TO 6

1 tbsp (15 g) tamarind paste

1½ lb (690 g) ground chicken breast

1 tbsp (15 ml) vegetable oil

3 cloves garlic, minced

1 large shallot, thinly sliced

2 oz (60 ml) fish sauce

2½ oz (75 ml) fresh lime juice

½ cup (100 g) palm sugar or brown sugar

1–2 tsp Thai chili powder

½ cup (20 g) mint leaves

½ red onion, thinly sliced

¼ cup (55 g) roasted rice powder

3–4 scallions, chopped

Stir the tamarind paste into the ground chicken in a large bowl and let it stand for 15 minutes.

Heat a medium pan to high heat and add oil. When you see the first wisps of white smoke, sauté the garlic and shallot until translucent, about 1 minute. Fold in the chicken and stir-fry until the chicken is just cooked through, about 3 to 4 minutes.

Turn off the heat then stir in the fish sauce, lime, sugar and chili powder and mix well. Adjust the flavors as necessary to your taste.

Fold in the mint, onion, roasted rice powder and scallions until well combined. Serve with carrot sticks, long bean, lettuce and cabbage all cut to about 4 to 5 inches (10 to 13 cm).

Pro Tips: If you can, have your butcher grind the chicken breast once using a large die. This will give you large chunks of chicken with texture instead of overly minced burger feel. Also, you can sub any meat or even tofu in this dish. Again, large die, single grind is the key.

Roasted rice powder is a fun condiment. It adds a great nutty, smoky crunch to larb and other dishes. It also soaks up the dressing and binds it to the dish, upping the flavor. I guarantee you have everything you need to make it at home, which is rice and a pan! Take about ½ cup (125 g) of white rice and roast it in a dry pan over medium-high heat. Keep stirring as the rice cooks. Once the rice is medium brown and fragrant, put it into a blender or food processor. Grind until a coarse powder is formed.

THAI BEEF SALAD (YUM NEAU)

This recipe is a great marinade for any meat you like to slap on the grill, like steaks, pork chops, or even lamb chops. And it's a great

Thai dressing that you can use on way more than just lettuces. You can use it on anything you would call a salad. The lemongrass and kaffir lime leaves can also be frozen. It's always tough to buy just a few leaves or stalks, so chop them fine and keep in a resealable plastic bag.

SERVES 4

Thai Grilled Beef Marinade

2 lb (900 g) beef flank steak

2 oz (60 g) minced garlic

2 oz (60 g) minced cilantro stems

1 tsp white pepper

2 tbsp (30 ml) fish sauce

1½ oz (45 ml) thin soy sauce

2 tbsp (30 g) sugar

Salad

2 tbsp (30 ml) peanut oil

3 cloves garlic, minced

1 stalk lemongrass, minced

3 kaffir lime leaves, very thinly sliced

½ cup (120 ml) lime juice

½ cup (120 ml) fish sauce

⅓ cup (75 g) brown sugar, packed

6 cups (255 g) mixed salad greens

½ red onion, thinly sliced

1 English cucumber, seeded and thinly sliced

2 green onions, chopped

½ cup (20 g) mint leaves

For the Marinade

Place the flank steak in a medium-large resealable bag or bowl. Add all the remaining ingredients on to the beef. Massage all the flavors into the beef for about 1 minute. Seal the bag and place it in the fridge for at least 2 hours to overnight.

For the Dressing

Heat a small saucepan over low heat. Add oil, garlic, lemongrass and kaffir lime leaves and sweat for 1 minute or until the garlic just starts to turn light brown. Remove from the heat and stir in the lime juice, fish sauce and brown sugar until thoroughly combined. Set aside.

For the Salad

Grill the marinated beef to your desired doneness and slice it against the grain into thin strips.

Add the salad greens, red onion and cucumbers with most of the dressing to a large bowl. Leave a few spoons of dressing for drizzling. Toss the salad gently to combine. Place the grilled beef on top of the salad and garnish it with the mint leaves and green onions. Drizzle the remaining dressing on top of the salad.

COCONUT MANGO SALAD WITH SHRIMP

Tart, sweet green mangoes are common in Thailand but hard to find in the States. These mangoes are evergreen; they never turn that yellowish orange color. I think green Granny Smith apples are the perfect replacement for this dish if needed. The tart, sweet crunch, complemented by the smoky coconut, pairs perfectly with plump shrimp.

SERVES 4

1 tbsp (15 ml) vegetable oil

½ lb (240 g) medium shrimp, sliced in half lengthwise

2 shallots, thinly sliced

2 cloves garlic, finely chopped

1–2 Thai chilies, thinly sliced

⅓ cup (80 ml) lime juice

⅓ cup (80 ml) fish sauce

½ cup (95 g) brown sugar or palm sugar

3 cups (720 g) matchstick-cut green mango

1 cup (75 g) toasted coconut chips

½ red onion, very thinly sliced

3 scallions, cut on the bias

¼ cup (35 g) cashew nuts, roasted

Heat a medium skillet on medium and add oil. When you see a wisp of white smoke, add the shrimp and lightly sauté them for about 1 minute, then reduce the heat to low. Add the shallots, garlic and Thai chilies and cook them for an additional minute, until the shrimp are just cooked through.

Turn off the heat. Stir in the lime juice, fish sauce and sugar. Stir it until the sugar is dissolved. Transfer the shrimp and dressing to a serving plate. Allow to cool for a few minutes. When ready to serve, arrange the mango, coconut and red onion in the serving bowl. Toss to combine, and garnish with scallions and cashews.

Pro Tip: You can buy unsweetened toasted coconut chips anywhere now and they are perfect for this recipe! If you can't get green mangoes, I would substitute julienned Granny Smith apples for half of the recipe for some tang and crunch.

CHILLED SESAME BROCCOLI SALAD

This is the perfect recipe when you need a delicious vegetable dish that's quick and easy. I think a lot of dressings are heavy and have too much oil or cream in them. This dressing is light, tangy and full of flavor but won't overwhelm you with oil. It's inspired by the soy and sesame Japanese dressings but with a hint of honey.

MAKES 6 TO 8 SERVINGS

¼ cup (60 ml) unseasoned rice wine vinegar

2 tbsp (30 ml) sesame oil

¼ cup (80 g) honey

3 tbsp (45 ml) soy sauce

2 lb (900 g) broccoli florets

2 tbsp (12 g) sesame seeds, toasted

Combine the rice wine vinegar, sesame oil, honey and soy sauce to make the dressing; set aside. May be prepped ahead for up to a week.

Bring about 2 quarts (1.8 L) of water to a rolling boil in a 4-quart (4.7-L) saucepan. Salt the water generously. Blanch the broccoli about 2 minutes, until it's al dente and bright green. Shock in a large bowl of ice water for about 3 minutes. Drain in a colander and reserve.

To serve, toss the chilled broccoli in a large bowl with the dressing until it's coated well. Sprinkle the broccoli with sesame seeds and serve.

CHINESE CHICKEN SALAD

I really wanted to add this recipe to the book because it's one of my favorites, and I guarantee that it will be one of the most popular dishes in your repertoire. You can also use just about any protein or none at all. This is a great dressing to just keep in the fridge because almost all bottled dressings suck. You can double this recipe, store it in a squeeze bottle and look extra cheffy.

MAKES 2½ CUPS (120 ML) OF DRESSING; SALAD SERVES 4 TO 6

Dressing

5 green onions (2" [5-cm]) white parts only, thinly sliced

1 tbsp (15 g) Chinese dry mustard, made into a paste by stirring in 1 tbsp (15 ml) water

⅓ cup (85 g) Japanese pickled ginger, packed

½ cup (120 ml) lime juice

1 tbsp (9 g) roughly chopped garlic

2 tbsp (20 g) roughly chopped shallots

½ cup (160 g) honey

⅔ cup (160 ml) Japanese soy sauce

⅓ cup (80 ml) rice vinegar

2 tbsp (16 g) roughly chopped ginger root

2 cups (480 ml) peanut oil

Salad

1 cup (240 g) canned tangerine segments, drained

5 cups (500 g) Napa cabbage

2 carrots, peeled and cut into thin strips

1 head radicchio, cut into thin strips

4 cups (170 g) mixed baby greens

2 lb (900 g) boneless, skinless chicken, cooked, cooled and diced

3 cups (711 ml) oil

5 wonton wrappers

2 tbsp (12 g) toasted sesame seeds

For the Dressing

Combine all the ingredients except the peanut oil in a blender. Blend them thoroughly for about 10 seconds, until no one item is recognizable. With the blender running, slowly drizzle in the peanut oil until the dressing is smooth and even. You can use immediately or store in an air-tight container for a week.

For the Salad

In a large salad bowl, toss the tangerines, cabbage, carrots, radicchio, greens and chicken.

Heat the oil in a small saucepan over medium-high heat. Cut the wonton skins into ¼-inch (6-mm) wide strips. When the oil reaches 365°F (185°C), fry until the strips are golden brown, about 30 seconds on each side. Drain the wonton strips on a paper towel and allow to cool. You'll need about 2 cups (90 g) of wonton strips. Toss them with the salad.

Toss your salad with 1 cup (240 ml) of the dressing. Add more dressing if needed, a little at a time. Sprinkle the salad with the sesame seeds and serve.

TOFU SALAD WITH TANGY SESAME DRESSING

I'll never understand people's fear of tofu. It's such a simple, delicious food. Low in calories, high in protein and very mild tasting. It takes the flavor of the dressing amazingly. This dressing is savory and tangy, with the smokiness of toasted sesame seeds. Paired with a glass of rosé, this is one of my favorite dishes for a warm day. If you are looking for a healthy but extremely satisfying dinner, pair this salad with my Cold Soba Noodles and you'll be transported right to Japan!

SERVES 4

Dressing

6 tbsp (48 g) Japanese sesame powder, or toasted sesame seeds

⅔ cup (160 g) mayonnaise

¼ cup (60 ml) rice vinegar

1 tbsp (8 g) minced ginger root

2 tbsp (30 ml) soy sauce

2 tbsp (30 ml) mirin

3 tbsp (45 ml) water

2 tsp (10 g) salt

3 tbsp (40 g) sugar

Salad

1 (14-oz [400-g]) carton medium tofu

1 small ripe plum or Roma tomato, sliced

1 small Japanese cucumber, sliced

¼ cup (10 g) daikon sprouts, bottoms trimmed

1 cup (12 g) bonito flakes (katsuobushi)

½ cup (40 g) thinly sliced nori

¼ cup (37 g) furikake topping

For the Dressing

Combine all the dressing ingredients in a blender and purée until smooth, about 30 seconds. Set the dressing aside in the refrigerator until ready to use.

For the Salad

Drain the tofu and pat it dry with paper towels. Cut the tofu in half lengthwise, making large planks, then place those planks in the middle of a serving plate. Arrange the tomato slices, cucumber slices and sprouts on top of the tofu. Drizzle about ¼ cup (60 ml) of dressing over the salad. Garnish with bonito flakes, nori and furikake.

CUCUMBER SEAWEED SALAD (SUNOMONO)

This recipe might seem simple but it's important. Anytime you've ordered a seaweed salad or cucumber salad in a Japanese restaurant, this dressing is the base! I make about a quart (946 ml) of this at a time, then when I have a craving for a clean Japanese salad, I cut up the vegetables, place them in a bowl and just pour this tangy, sweet dressing over them.

SERVES 4

Cucumber Seaweed Salad Dressing

1 cup (240 ml) rice vinegar

½ cup (100 g) sugar

½ tsp salt

Salad

1 English cucumber

½ cup (62 g) salt

¼ cup (40 g) dried wakame seaweed

Sesame seeds, for garnish

Daikon sprouts, for garnish

For the Dressing

Heat the vinegar in a small saucepan over low heat until warm. Stir in the sugar and salt and whisk constantly until solids have completely dissolved.

For the Salad

Slice the cucumber in half lengthwise. Scoop out the seeds, then slice the cucumber into ⅛-inch (3-mm) half-moon slices and place in a small bowl. Sprinkle the salt over the cucumber slices and wait about 5 to 10 minutes. This will draw out a lot of the moisture in the cucumber, making it very crispy. Wash off the salt and allow to drain well.

In a small saucepan, heat 3 cups (705 ml) of water to a simmer and turn off the heat. Add the wakame seaweed and allow it to bloom and fully reconstitute. Once soft, rinse it with cold water and roughly chop it. Drain the seaweed very well.

Combine the cucumbers and seaweed in a bowl and dress to serve. Garnish with the sesame seeds and daikon.

DUMPLINGS, FINGER FOODS AND SMALL PLATES

I can't think of an Asian culture that doesn't love to graze. It's rare to eat fixed courses in a progressive meal except for maybe Japanese Kaiseki. All dishes are fair game to be eaten at any meal period, and many meals are eaten family style. As a kid being raised and taught to cook by my mom's mom, who was Cantonese, I started thousands of days eating dim sum. Along with dumplings, my family loved to graze on small dishes we liked to call knick-knacks.

This chapter features some of my favorite knick-knacks and dim sum dishes. As you progress through this book, I'll break down the chapters by technique and meal periods. And I should reiterate, this is an Asian cookbook, so you will find dishes from all over Asia.

A lot of these dishes were handed down directly from my grandmother and other family members. They are tried and tested and are a product of hundreds of years of combined experience. Other recipes are from my travels and years of cooking with home cooks, chefs, street vendors and anyone who had knowledge they wanted to part with. These recipes are like my kids; I've loved them, raised them and am very proud to share them with you!

VIETNAMESE CRYSTAL SHRIMP SPRING ROLLS

These Vietnamese spring rolls are classic fresh uncooked rolls with soft rice skins. This version is my favorite, but you can fill this wrap with a variety of proteins and vegetables if you want to try something different. My other favorite is the Vietnamese Crispy Imperial Roll. The secret to holding these rolls to eat later is to place a moist paper towel, then a piece of plastic wrap, between layers. Rice papers can be found in many shapes and sizes. I like using the 8-inch (20-cm) papers. Make sure to check the package for cracks in the papers. You can't mend them, so buy whole, unbroken papers.

MAKES 8 ROLLS

Hoisin Peanut Dipping Sauce

½ cup (120 ml) hoisin sauce

3 tbsp (45 g) creamy peanut butter

4 tbsp (60 ml) water

1 tbsp (15 ml) rice vinegar

Spring Rolls

4 oz (95 g) rice vermicelli noodles

1 medium carrot, peeled and julienned

2 cups (85 g) shredded lettuce

8 (8″ [20-cm]) round rice paper sheets

½ cup (25 g) Vietnamese basil leaves

½ cup (25 g) fresh cilantro leaves

8 oz (240 g) cooked, peeled shrimp, cut in half lengthwise

For the Sauce
Combine the sauce ingredients, then set aside until ready to serve.

For the Spring Rolls

Cook the rice vermicelli noodles in boiling water for about 5 minutes, or until al dente. Shock them in ice water to stop the cooking process, and drain them well.

Combine the noodles, carrot and lettuce to make the filling.

Soak the rice paper in warm water for about 15 seconds, until it starts to soften, and then place it on your cutting board. Place about ½ cup (25 g) of the vegetable filling in the center of the wrapper and top it with the basil, cilantro and two shrimp pieces.

Roll from the bottom up, containing the filling with your fingers. Once the bottom skin rolls over once, push down to flatten it a little. Fold in two sides snugly, and then roll up the parcel. Lay it seam-side down on a serving plate. Serve with the Hoisin Peanut Dipping Sauce.

VIETNAMESE CRISPY IMPERIAL ROLLS

There's been a growing confusion over the past 40 years about the difference between Vietnamese spring rolls and Chinese egg rolls.

Vietnam was ruled by China for over 1,000 years, and they traded a lot of food influences. The Vietnamese took the Chinese egg roll and, in my opinion, made it perfect. These are the Vietnamese thin-skinned rolls filled with savory ground pork, springy noodles and crispy carrots. They are always served with a sauce named nuoc mam—a thinner version of sweet chili sauce. Chinese egg rolls are thick-skinned, loaded primarily with vegetables and eat doughy and heavy.

MAKES 12 ROLLS

Filling

3 tbsp (45 g) dried wood ear mushrooms

2–3 cups (280–420 g) bean thread noodles

1 lb (450 g) ground pork butt

2 cloves garlic, finely minced

4 shallots, minced

3 tbsp (45 g) sugar

3 tbsp (45 ml) fish sauce

Pinch pepper

1 cup (50 g) grated carrot

1 cup (35 g) bean sprouts

Rolls

12 (8″ [20-cm]) round spring roll wrappers

2 qt (1.8 L) vegetable oil for deep-frying

12 romaine heart leaves

½ bunch fresh mint leaves

½ bunch cilantro leaves

Nuoc Cham Dipping Sauce

For the Filling

Reconstitute the mushrooms by soaking in hot water for 20 to 30 minutes. Drain and cut them into fine julienne.

Cook the bean thread noodles in boiling water until al dente, about 3 to 5 minutes. Rinse the noodles under running water, which stops the cooking process. Drain well in a colander and let drip dry until completely cooled.

In a large bowl, knead the filling ingredients well until thoroughly combined and set aside.

For the Rolls

Pull the spring roll wrappers apart gently. To wrap, lay the wrapper in a diamond shape with a point at 6 o'clock.

Place about 3 to 4 tablespoons (15 to 20 g) of the filling in the lower half of the wrapper. Roll it over twice to make a tight log; then bring in the sides to make a package similar to an envelope. Continue to roll until it ends. Place it on a lightly oiled surface. Continue to make rolls until no filling remains.

Add oil to a 5-quart (4.7-L) Dutch oven or pot and place over high heat. When the temperature reaches 375°F (191°C), fry the rolls until they reach a light golden color or internal temperature reaches 165°F (74°C). Serve with a plate of lettuce leaves, herbs and Nuoc Cham Dipping Sauce.

Pro Tip: To eat like a pro, wrap an imperial roll in a lettuce leaf, stuff in a few herbs of choice like mint or cilantro and drench in sauce.

VIETNAMESE BANH MI SANDWICH

Banh mi are the hottest sandwiches in America and you don't have to find a Vietnamese banh mi shop to enjoy one. You have most of the ingredients at any decently stocked market in America! The trick here is to make the roasted shaved pork at home. The secret is brining the pork before roasting! You can use chicken breast in this recipe as well. Try to find very light, airy baguettes or French rolls. A good banh mi should be crispy on the outside and light and airy in the middle. Stay away from the bread that will shred the roof of your mouth!

MAKES 1 VERY LONG SANDWICH OR 3 SMALL ONES

Roast Pork

10 cups (2.4 L) water, divided

½ cup (124 g) kosher salt

½ cup (95 g) granulated sugar

3 medium cloves garlic, peeled

1 medium serrano chile, crushed

1 tbsp (15 g) black peppercorns, cracked

1½ lb (625 g) boneless pork shoulder

Pickled Carrots

½ cup (120 ml) distilled white vinegar

½ cup (95 g) granulated sugar

1 tsp kosher salt

1½ cups (75 g) matchstick-cut carrots

Banh Mi

1 French baguette (not sourdough)

¼ cup (60 ml) mayonnaise, divided

3 oz (90 g) pork pâté (optional)

1 large English cucumber, shaved into ribbons with a peeler

¼ cup (10 g) cilantro leaves

1 jalapeño, sliced very thin

2 tsp (10 ml) light soy sauce

For the Pork

To make the brine, bring 2 cups (470 ml) of water to a simmer in a small saucepan. Stir in the salt and sugar and keep stirring or whisking until all the solids have completely dissolved. Turn off the heat and add the garlic, chilies and peppercorns to the saucepan. The heat will make all their flavors open up. Pour the warm brine into a 6-quart (5.7-L) nonreactive container large enough to hold the pork and 10 cups (2.4 L) of liquid. Pour in the remaining 8 cups (1.8 L) of cold water. Add your pork, cover and refrigerate overnight.

Preheat your oven to 400°F (204°C) and arrange a rack in the middle. Remove the pork from the brine, use paper towels to pat it very dry and place fat-side up in a roasting pan. Allow it to come to room temperature for about 30 minutes. Roast the pork until the internal temperature reaches 165°F (74°C), about 1 hour 45 minutes. Let it cool to room temperature, at least 45 minutes, then slice thinly, about ⅛-inch (3-mm) thick.

For the Pickled Carrots

Combine the vinegar, sugar and salt in a small saucepan over medium heat. Stir constantly, and once the sugar and salt have dissolved, remove it from the heat. Add the carrots, and stir to coat them in the pickling mixture. Let stand until the carrots have softened, at least 30 minutes or overnight. Drain them well and set aside. You can make this days ahead and keep refrigerated in an airtight container.

To Assemble the Banh Mi

Slice off the top third of the baguette lengthwise and set aside. Remove enough of the bottom interior of the bread so the filling can fit easily.

Spread 2 tablespoons (28 g) of the mayonnaise on the top part and 2 tablespoons (28 g) on the bottom. Spread half of the pâté on the bottom section and top it with the sliced pork. There may be some left over, so smash it into your mouth and enjoy while building the banh mi. Then continue to build with the cucumber, cilantro leaves, pickled carrots and jalapeños. Sprinkle sandwich with a few drops of soy sauce and close with the upper half of the baguette.

Pro Tip: Combine the pâté and mayo in a food processor to make a spread. You can also sub in cold cuts here for the roast pork to save a step. You can also sub out half the carrots for daikon radish for some extra deliciousness.

SWEET CHILI SRIRACHA HOT WINGS

It's no secret that my food vice is fried chicken wings. If I had no self-control, I'd eat about 10 pounds (4.5 kg) a day. Not just any though; these are my famous sweet and hot wings. It's the perfect balance between sweet, hot, and savory. Using tempura flour will give you a super crunchy exterior that will soak up this great sauce.

SERVES 4 TO 6

3 cups (720 ml) Thai sweet chili sauce

¾ cup (120 ml) Sriracha, or more if you prefer it spicier

12 whole chicken wings, cut in half at the joint, with tips discarded

2 cups (250 g) tempura flour

2.5 qt (2.8 L) vegetable oil, for frying

2 cups (224 g) cornstarch

Make the sauce by stirring together the sweet chili sauce and Sriracha in a large bowl. You will be frying the wings and rolling them into this sauce while hot.

Rinse the chicken wings in cold water, drain them briefly and then place them in a shallow baking dish still wet. Sprinkle the wings evenly with the tempura flour, and massage until a thin batter forms.

Place oil in a 6-quart (5.7-L) Dutch oven or pot and heat on high. Bring the temperature of the oil to 365°F (185°C).

Pour the cornstarch into a separate large bowl. Dredge the chicken wings, dust off the excess and fry the wings in three batches. Cook each batch for 8 to 10 minutes, turning occasionally, until cooked through and golden brown. The internal temperature should be 165°F (74°C).

Drain the wings on paper towels briefly and roll them in the prepared sauce. Serve hot.

THAI SAVORY PORK JERKY (MOO DAT DIOW)

I like to call this dish "pork crack" because you will be addicted to these sweet, savory nuggets! It's a great snack by itself or eaten with Thai sticky rice as a meal. It also travels incredibly well because it's glazed with soy and sugar and fried. I pack it for long trips and for my kids' lunches.

SERVES 4

1 lb (450 g) pork shoulder

1 clove garlic, minced

1 tsp white pepper

2 tbsp (30 ml) fish sauce

1 tbsp (15 ml) Thai soybean sauce (aka Maggi seasoning sauce)

2 tbsp (30 ml) sweet soy sauce

1 tbsp (15 g) brown sugar

1 qt (946 ml) vegetable oil, for frying

Cut the pork into thin strips about 3-inch (7.5-cm) long and ½-inch (12-mm) wide. It's OK to trim any silver skin away, but don't trim too much fat off.

Combine all the ingredients except the pork in a blender and blend them into a fine purée or until you can't detect any garlic bits in the marinade.

Place the pork in a bowl, pour the marinade over the pork and massage it well until the pork is completely coated. Marinate the pork, covered, in the refrigerator for 4 hours to overnight.

Line a cookie sheet with paper towels or parchment paper. Blot off excess marinade, lay the pork on the sheet pan and allow it to dry in the fridge overnight.

Heat about 1 quart (946 ml) of vegetable oil in a medium saucepan on high. Bring the temperature up to about 375°F (191°C), and fry the pork strips in small batches. Cook for about 4 to 6 minutes, until cooked through and edges are slightly crisp. Remove the pork from the heat and drain on paper towels.

HAWAIIAN OG TUNA POKE

Poke is a Hawaiian snack dish made from super fresh sushi-grade fish. The Hawaiian fishermen would sell off the prime cuts to market and keep the perfectly delicious scraps to themselves and make poke. Poke comes from the Hawaiian verb "to cut." Traditional poke is made either with tuna or octopus. It's important to buy fish from a place you trust and make sure it's sushi quality. Make this dish ahead and enjoy it as an appetizer or get creative! It's super cool to make mashup burritos or top salads with it.

SERVES 4

1 lb (454 g) sushi-grade tuna

¼ cup (20 g) dried wakame seaweed

⅓ cup (35 g) finely diced Sweet Maui or Vidalia onion

1 tsp sesame oil

½ tsp chili flakes (if you like a little heat)

2 tsp (10 ml) soy sauce

½ tbsp (4 g) toasted sesame seeds

2 scallions, cut thinly on the bias

Place 1 cup (240 ml) hot water in a bowl and gently rain in the wakame; let it reconstitute. Rinse under cold water, squeeze out the water with your hands and it's ready to use. Cut the tuna into tidy ½-inch (12-mm) cubes and transfer to a cold bowl. The cold bowl keeps the raw fish cold.

Add the wakame, onion, sesame oil, chili flakes and soy sauce. Use a large spoon to fold very gently, like you're folding egg whites, until everything is well combined. Garnish with sesame seeds and scallions.

*See photo.

*See photo.

> **Pro Tip:** Make sure to wash your hands well before making this dish and throughout the preparation process.

VEGETABLE AND SHRIMP TEMPURA

Tempura is like pizza, it's all pretty darn good, even the mediocre stuff. But, like pizza, when you eat really amazing tempura, it's transformative! Great tempura is characterized by a super light batter that is very crispy and not greasy. One secret is building the crust as it's frying, like double-crusting fried chicken. All those extra little hanging bits of crust double the crunch. The secret is in this recipe my friends!

SERVES 4

---

1 recipe Tempura Dipping Sauce

8 medium shrimp

1 medium onion, peeled

4 shiitake mushrooms or white mushrooms, wiped and trimmed

1 small sweet potato

4 shiso leaves

1 egg yolk

1 cup (240 ml) ice water

½ cup (120 g) sifted flour

½ cup (60 g) cornstarch

2 qt (1.8 L) oil for deep-frying

2 cups (224 g) cornstarch for dredging

Warm the dipping sauce over heat, bringing just to a boil. Keep warm.

Shell and devein the shrimp, but leave the tails attached. To prevent the shrimp from curling as they are deep-fried, make a few deep incisions along the curve of the back. Squeeze the shrimp until you feel the flesh squish and stretch the shrimp out.

Pierce the onions with toothpicks to hold the slices together, then cut into rounds.

If the mushroom caps are very large, cut them in half. Peel the sweet potato and slice it crosswise into ¼-inch (6-mm) rounds.

Wash and pat dry the shiso leaves with paper towels.

In a large mixing bowl, lightly beat one egg yolk and ice water together. Add the flour and cornstarch all at once. Stroke a few times with chopsticks or fork, just until the ingredients are loosely combined. The batter should be very lumpy. If you overmix it, the batter will be more like that for fish and chips.

Heat your oil in a 4-quart (3.8-L) saucepan. The oil should be fairly hot, about 350°F (177°C). Test it by dropping a tiny bit of batter into the oil; it should sink and bubble up almost immediately and crackle.

Create an assembly line with the fryer in the middle. On the left, the raw items to be fried, then the dredging cornstarch in a medium bowl, then oil in the center. To the right a draining area like a wire rack over a sheet tray. Use tongs to move food out of the fryer and a small strainer would help for fishing out extra crispy tempura batter.

To fry, use your fingers to dip food into the dredging cornstarch, shake off the excess, then dip it in the batter. Lay or slide the coated food in the hot oil. As the crust starts to form and harden, go back into the batter with your thumb, index and middle fingers together. Gather some extra batter and drizzle it over the frying piece of food. The motion is like sprinkling salt over food. This little extra umph adds those uneven bits of batter that make tempura look lumpy and add crunch. Deep-fry until golden, about 3 minutes, turning in the oil for even cooking. Retrieve it with a slotted spoon or cooking chopsticks, and briefly drain it before transferring it to a serving plate. Skim the surface of the oil occasionally to keep it clean. Stir the batter once or twice as you work, to keep it from separating.

DIM SUM DRUM DUMPLING (SEW MAI)

Dim sum literally translates to "fill the heart." I love filling my belly with this Cantonese breakfast! It originated in little tea houses in southern China that served steamed and fried bites with your choice of tea and is the modern version of a culinary swap meet. Masses of people all competing for fresh cooked bites of food auctioned off carts. These are my favorite type of dumpling. Shaped like drums, stuffed with shrimp and pork, they are the best.

MAKES ABOUT 8 TO 10 DUMPLINGS

5 dried Chinese black mushrooms

¾ lb (340 g) coarsely ground pork butt

½ lb (240 g) shrimp, peeled, deveined and coarsely chopped

½ tsp salt

2 tsp (10 g) sugar

½ tbsp (8 ml) peanut oil

1½ tbsp (22 ml) oyster sauce

1 tsp cornstarch

1 tbsp (15 ml) sesame oil

Pinch white pepper

1 package Hong Kong–style round dumpling skins

Reconstitute the mushrooms in hot water for 30 minutes. Rinse them, remove the stems and chop them into small dice.

In a large bowl, combine the remainder of the filling ingredients and mix until well combined. You may also use a mixer with a paddle attachment for this. Cover the mixture and let it rest in the refrigerator for at least an hour to overnight.

Lay a dumpling skin on your work surface. Place about 2 tablespoons (15 g) of filling in the center. Hold the filling in place with your fingers and use the other hand to twist the skin around the filling. While twisting, make sure to flatten the top of the filling into the skin. Place the bottom of the dumpling on the work surface and flatten it out. Repeat this process until all the filling is gone.

Steam the dumplings in a steamer basket on high for about 7 minutes or until cooked through.

Pro Tip: I love eating these with my grandma's not-so-secret sauce, which is just equal parts soy sauce, chili garlic sauce and sugar.

FIVE—SPICE PORK BELLY SLIDERS

Bao buns are one of my favorite snacks! These are the empty versions of those super white pillowy buns you get at dim sum places, usually filled with chopped BBQ pork. They are shaped like a thick eye patch with a seam in the middle you can pull open and stuff. They are readily available at any Chinese market in the frozen section.

MAKES 12 BUNS

---

2 lb (900 g) pork belly

2 tbsp (30 ml) vegetable oil

4 scallions, cut into 3″ (7.5-cm) lengths

2 fingers off a large hand of unpeeled ginger, cut into slices

Water to cover

¾ cup (180 ml) oyster sauce

½ cup (120 ml) light soy sauce

¼ cup (60 ml) hoisin sauce

½ cup (95 g) brown sugar

2 tbsp (30 g) five-spice powder

16 bao buns (aka frozen folded mantou steamed buns)

8 scallions, julienne cut into 4″ (10-cm) lengths and soaked in ice water until curly

4–6 oz (90–120 ml) hoisin sauce

Preheat the oven to 325°F (165°C). Make sure to arrange a rack that's under the middle with enough room for the Dutch oven.

Cut the pork into long strips that are 4-inches (10-cm) wide. Strips should be wide enough to fit into the bun.

In a large Dutch oven, heat 2 tablespoons (30 ml) of oil until you see the first wisps of white smoke. Place the pork belly skin-side down and cook for about 3 to 5 minutes on each side, until nice and brown.

Add the scallions and ginger and fry them until fragrant, about 2 minutes. Add enough water just to cover the pork.

Stir in the oyster sauce, light soy, hoisin sauce, brown sugar and five-spice powder and stir them all to combine. Bring the mixture to a boil, then reduce to a simmer. Cover loosely with foil, then put the lid on.

Place in the oven and bake for 3 hours until fork-tender. Remove from the oven and allow to cool, reserve the liquid and skim off the fat.

To assemble the bao, slice the pork into ¼-inch (6-mm) wide tiles. Steam or fry the buns until they're hot and open, and then place the pork and scallions inside. Finish the pork belly buns with about a teaspoon of hoisin sauce.

Pro Tip: If you can't find the bao buns in the store, I like using small Hawaiian rolls or slider-sized buns to make these.

CRAB RANGOON—CREAM CHEESE CRAB WONTON

Ok, I know what you're thinking: WTF is crab rangoon doing in the book? BUT WAIT! As an American-born Asian kid, I grew up eating items that were created in the States but are authentic in flavors. The Chinese have been here since the 1800s and if dishes were created by Asians in America I think they are totally authentic. Dishes like orange chicken, California roll, spicy tuna and crab rangoon have now made their way back to the Asian countries from which their native creators originated.

MAKES 24 PIECES

8 oz (227 g) lump crab meat or snow crab

16 oz (454 g) cream cheese, room temp

2 green onions (whites only), very finely chopped

2 tbsp (5 g) finely chopped tarragon

Salt and pepper

24 wonton skins (square)

1 egg, slightly beaten, for sealing

2 qt (1.9 L) vegetable oil for frying

Press out as much liquid as possible from any crab meat you are using. Any excess moisture will soak through the wonton skins. In a medium bowl combine the crab, cream cheese, green onion, tarragon, salt and pepper either with your hands or a mixer with a paddle attachment.

Take a wonton skin, place 1 teaspoon of filling in the center of each wrapper. With a finger dipped in egg, moisten the 2 adjacent sides;

fold over the opposing corner to make a triangle.

You have some choices with shape. You can make a purse, tortellini or traditional triangle wontons.

Place the completed ones on a tray. Uncooked, rangoons can be wrapped and kept frozen for 1 to 2 weeks and dropped into the fryer frozen.

Heat oil in a 4- or 5-quart (3.8- or 4.7-L) Dutch oven or pot until the oil reaches 360°F (182°C). Fry in small batches until golden about 2 minutes on each side and drain on a wire rack over a cookie sheet. I like to serve these with sweet chili or plum sauce.

SUGARCANE CRISPY SHRIMP

This is a great appetizer to serve when you want to impress your friends. It looks like a crispy shrimp fritter wrapped around a sugarcane spear. You wrap it in a lettuce leaf, slather on sauce and before you eat it, slide it off the cane. You can leave out the spear if you want and just shape it into little round fritters, similar to donut holes. I love eating these with my Nuoc Cham Sauce, plum sauce or sweet chili sauce.

MAKES ABOUT 8 PIECES

4 cloves garlic, finely chopped

2 lb (900 g) shrimp, cleaned and peeled

2 tsp (10 g) sugar

1 whole egg

½ cup (95 g) ground pork

2 tbsp (30 g) roasted rice, ground

1 piece sugarcane, cut into 4 equal pieces about 4" (10 cm) long by ½" (12-mm) thick

1½ qt (1.8 L) vegetable oil for deep frying

8 leaves green leaf lettuce

Load the garlic, shrimp, sugar, egg, pork and rice into a large food processor. Pulse it all until you get a uniform but still semi-chunky paste. With lightly oiled hands, form 3 tablespoons (100 g) of the shrimp mixture into oval balls. Press each ball around a sugarcane spear. Repeat until all the shrimp mixture is used.

Heat the oil in a 6-quart (5.7 L) Dutch oven or pot. Preheat the oil to 370°F (188°C). Fry the shrimp fritters in two batches until golden brown, about 3 minutes on each side.

Serve each skewer wrapped in lettuce with plum sauce. Make sure your diners remove the skewer before eating the shrimp.

Pro Tips: If you can't find sugarcane sticks at the stores, try using lemongrass stalks. Sugarcane can also be found in cans and cut into quarters lengthwise for perfect skewers. You can also just shape this into patties and make shrimp fritters.

Roasted rice powder can be bought in the store, but making it yourself is fun and easy. Take about ½ cup (125 g) of white rice and roast it in a dry pan over medium-high heat. Keep stirring as the rice cooks. Once the rice is medium brown and fragrant, put it into a blender or food processor. Grind until a coarse powder is formed.

MINCED CHICKEN LETTUCE CUPS WITH HOISIN SAUCE

Did you know minced chicken in lettuce cups has a history that ties to Peking duck? After the carver deftly peels away the airy, crispy skin and serves it to you with the crepes or buns in hoisin sauce, they'll usually ask you what you want done with the 95 percent of what's left, the delicious carcass. My favorite way to use it is this dish right here.

SERVES 4

Stir-Fry Sauce
2 tbsp (30 ml) hoisin sauce

1 tbsp (15 ml) soy sauce

2 tbsp (30 ml) oyster sauce

2 tbsp (30 ml) water

1 tsp sesame oil

1 tsp sugar

1 tsp cornstarch mixed with 1 tsp water

Lettuce Cups
1 tsp cornstarch

2 tsp (10 ml) sherry

2 tsp (10 ml) water

1½ lb (690 g) coarsely ground chicken (see tip)

2 tbsp (30 ml) vegetable oil

1 tsp minced ginger

2 cloves garlic, minced

8 fresh shiitake mushrooms, sliced thin

1 (8-oz [240-g]) can water chestnuts, diced

1 head butter lettuce leaves

2 green onions, sliced

For the Sauce

Mix all the ingredients for the sauce in a bowl, and set aside.

For the Lettuce Cups

In a medium bowl, combine the cornstarch, sherry, water and chicken. Stir it well to coat the chicken thoroughly. Let it sit for at least 20 minutes.

Heat a wok or large skillet over high heat for about a minute. Add oil and wait for the first wisps of white smoke. Add the chicken and stir-fry it for about 2 to 3 minutes, until the chicken is opaque and mostly cooked through.

Stir in the ginger and garlic, and stir-fry for about a minute, until the garlic is starting to brown.

Add the mushrooms and water chestnuts, and stir-fry an additional minute, until the mushrooms start to soften. Add the cooking sauce to the pan, constantly folding until the sauce starts to thicken. Spoon chicken into the lettuce leaf and roll. Serve by filling a lettuce leaf with about ½ cup (100 g) of chicken and garnish with green onions. Hoisin is the perfect sauce for the table.

Pro Tip: Not all ground meats are the same. First, which muscle? I'm not a huge fan of chicken breast, because it's dry and bland, but it's perfect for this dish for those reasons. It will stay together and not feel mushy and soaks up all the flavors of the sauce and vegetables. The "die" is a disc that has little holes inside it. Once the chicken is ground, it's pressed through the die, which helps size the grind. I like using a large die to keep the grind chunky and meaty. Lastly, most meat is ground twice to make sure the size is even. I think that makes ground meat too mealy and liquid. So if you have a great butcher, always ask for large-die, single-ground meat, and you'll have a superior product.

SWEETS
THE TASTIEST WAY TO END ANY DAY

If you have watched me cook or judge on TV, you know desserts are not my strong suit. I've lost national TV shows to home cooks because my pastry skills are so-so. In fact, I almost dropped out of culinary school because of my poor baking marks. I think it's because Asians approach desserts very differently, especially in Thailand, China and Japan.

Dairy has not traditionally been part of the food culture, and without dairy, you miss so many things. There's no milk, cream or butter, which means there's no ice cream or chocolate! I know it's hard to imagine. What we do have is a rich culture of making fruit, rice and coconuts into amazing desserts, and I will show you some of those in this chapter. I know what I like, and I can cook the hell out of the following recipes. These are my tested tried-and-true sweet recipes. Ali Tila is the family baker for sure, and I've included one of her amazing creations. The rest are dishes I've learned over the years.

COCONUT STICKY RICE WITH MANGO

Mangoes are available almost all year long in Thailand, and there is never a shortage of rice. Here is a sinful dessert that joins the two. I know rice is rarely considered a dessert food, but this is a delicious treat. Coconut sticky rice can be eaten with any fruit and is great by itself. Thai sweet rice, not jasmine, is used to make this dish. What makes the rice stick together is its high starch content. Sweet rice is actually steamed instead of simmered. This is a special dessert, and like all things that taste sinful, it is to be enjoyed in moderation. Manila mangos are in season in the States for about 3 to 4 months out of the year. Their extra sweetness and soft texture make them a perfect accompaniment to the coconut sticky rice.

SERVES 4 TO 6

---

3 cups (640 g) Thai sweet rice

2 cups (480 ml) coconut milk

1–1½ cups (200–300 g) granulated sugar

1 tsp salt

4 Manila mangoes, sliced into thin long pieces

Soak the sweet rice covered in water for at least 3 hours, preferably overnight.

Transfer the soaked rice into a bamboo basket. The rice should sit on the bottom of the basket. Add 4 cups (960 ml) of water into the steamer pot. Heat the water on high until it's boiling.

Insert the basket into the pot and cover it for 10 minutes. Flip the rice once and let it steam for another 10 minutes.

Heat the coconut milk, sugar and salt in a small saucepan until simmering, then remove it from the heat. Reserve ¼ cup (60 ml) and fold the remaining coconut sauce into rice. Cover the rice for 30 minutes.

When ready to serve, drizzle the reserved coconut sauce over the rice, and serve with very ripe mangoes or any fruit in season.

FRIED BANANAS

I think every culture that has bananas has a fried version. The most famous are Cuban maduros and tostones, but these will give them a

run for their money. What makes these magical is the Thai twist of adding shredded coconut to the sweetened batter. It's kind of like making a donut batter around a banana. These are crazy good!

SERVES 4

---

2 qt (1.9 L) vegetable oil for frying

6 firm ripe bananas

¾ cup (180 ml) water

2 eggs, beaten

2 tbsp (30 g) sugar

½ cup (65 g) all-purpose flour

2 tbsp (16 g) cornstarch

½ cup (40 g) shredded coconut

1 tsp toasted sesame seeds

Heat a large Dutch oven or heavy pot to high and add the oil. Heat the oil to 365°F (185°C).

Peel the bananas and cut them in half lengthwise, then in half crosswise.

Whisk together the water and eggs until combined. Stir in the sugar, flour, cornstarch, coconut and sesame seeds until just combined—some lumps are OK. To keep the batter light and crispy, don't overwork it.

Roll the bananas in the batter and shake off any excess; fry immediately. Fry until golden brown on one side, about 2 minutes. Turn, then fry an additional 1 to 2 minutes on the other side. Drain on a wire rack and serve warm.

CINNAMON AND FIVE—SPICE EASY DONUTS

Anything that makes your life easy, I would never call a cheat. I like to call them hacks! This is a great donut hack. I could eat donuts until my waistline and heart exploded, but making them isn't an easy process. Freezer biscuits make the perfect quick and simple donut batter. They are yeasty, sweet and pillowy and fry up perfectly. If you want the traditional ring-shaped donut, roll them with a rolling pin and punch a hole in the middle of each donut. But I usually just flatten them out and cut them in half or quarters to make more of a beignet shape.

MAKES 16 SMALL DONUTS

2 tsp (4 g) ground five-spice powder

2 tbsp (16 g) ground cinnamon

½ cup (95 g) sugar

2 cups (227 g) confectioners' sugar

¼ cup (60 ml) milk

1 tsp vanilla extract

1 (16-oz [454-g]) can large buttermilk biscuits

2 qt (1.8 L) vegetable oil, plus more as needed

In a large bowl, stir together the five-spice, ground cinnamon and sugar and set it aside. To make the glaze, whisk together the confectioners' sugar, milk and vanilla extract until the glaze is smooth and even.

Lay out the biscuits on a cutting board and cut them in half. Heat the oil to 365°F (185°C) in a 4-quart (3.8-L) Dutch oven. Fry the donuts in the oil for about 2 minutes on each side or until golden. Drain them on a wire rack over a sheet pan for about 2 minutes. Immediately dip one side in the glaze and top it with the spiced sugar.

GREEN TEA ICE CREAM

Although dairy isn't common, this is the perfect mash-up of Asian and western culture. I love making homemade ice cream. I think by using great milk, cream and eggs, you get a better product, not to mention brownie points from your guests and family. Make sure you are buying a green tea powder also known as matcha powder and not green tea leaves. It's a common mistake. The powder is super fine and will mix into anything, like ice cream and lattes!

MAKES 1 QUART (946 ML)

2 cups (480 ml) heavy cream

2 cups (480 ml) half-and-half

1 tsp vanilla extract

9 egg yolks

¾ cup (150 g) sugar

2 tbsp (20 g) green tea powder

In a medium saucepan over medium heat, combine the cream, half-and-half and vanilla, stirring occasionally to make sure the mixture doesn't scorch on the bottom. When the cream mixture reaches a simmer (do not let it boil), remove from the heat.

In a medium bowl, whisk together the egg yolks and sugar. Whisking constantly, slowly ladle in the hot cream mixture little by little. Congrats, you've just made a custard!

Return the custard mixture back to the saucepan and cook it over medium heat, stirring constantly with a wooden spoon. At 160°F (71°C), the mixture will give off a puff of steam. When the mixture reaches 180°F (82°C), it will be thickened and creamy, like eggnog. If you don't have a thermometer, test it by dipping a wooden spoon into the mixture. Run your finger down the back of the spoon. If the line from your finger remains clear, the mixture is ready; if the edges blur, the mixture is not quite thick enough yet.

Quickly remove it from the heat and whisk in the green tea powder until completely combined. Place the contents into a metal bowl and chill in the refrigerator until completely cool, about 4 hours to overnight. Now follow the directions of your ice cream maker of choice and enjoy!

ALI'S COCONUT RICE PUDDING

My wife, Ali, does almost all of the baking and dessert-making in our house. I wanted to add this because it is one of my favorites and a fab dessert. Use a good-quality Thai coconut milk, and remember, light coconut milk is a joke. It's like buying fat-free ice cream: it totally defeats the purpose and flavor!

SERVES 4

1 cup (75 g) sweetened coconut

1¼ cups (300 ml) canned unsweetened coconut milk, shaken or stirred

1½ cups (375 g) cooked jasmine rice (day-old rice works well here)

2¼ cups (535 ml) whole milk

⅓ cup (67 g) sugar

¼ tsp salt

½–1 tsp vanilla bean paste (or vanilla extract)

Heat a medium skillet over medium heat. Add the sweetened coconut and toast it until it's golden brown. Remove the coconut from the pan and set aside.

In a medium saucepan over medium heat, combine the coconut milk, rice, whole milk and sugar. Cook the pudding until it's thickened, stirring frequently for about 45 minutes. Add salt and vanilla bean paste, and stir to combine. Garnish your pudding with the toasted coconut and serve.

8 TREASURE RICE PUDDING

This is a traditional Chinese New Year dessert. The eight treasures are lucky and symbolize riches and magic charms that bring fortune for the New Year. Eight is also a very auspicious number in the Chinese culture. So you can see why this is so lucky! Make sure to use short-grain glutinous rice for this recipe.

SERVES 4 TO 6

Pudding

1 oz (30 g) lotus seeds

2 cups (480 ml) cold water

2 oz (50 g) Chinese red dates

2 cups (480 g) glutinous rice

¼ cup (50 g) sugar

3 tbsp (45 ml) vegetable oil, divided

1 red maraschino cherry, stemmed

1 cup (225 g) candied fruit

1 cup (240 g) red bean paste

Sweet Almond Sauce

3 tbsp (45 g) sugar

1 cup (240 ml) water

1 tsp almond extract

1 tbsp (8 g) cornstarch mixed with

1 tbsp (15 ml) water

For the Pudding

Add the lotus seeds to the cold water in a saucepan and bring to a boil. Simmer on low heat for 20 minutes. Drain the seeds and cool. Split them into halves and set aside.

Put the red dates in a bowl on a rack in a pot or steamer. Steam them, covered, over boiling water for 30 minutes. Set aside.

Put the rice in a pot and fill with water until it reaches ¾ inch (18 mm) above the rice. Bring it to a boil. Simmer it for 20 minutes. Stir in the sugar and 2 tablespoons (30 ml) of oil. Mix well and set aside.

Grease a medium-sized bowl heavily with remaining tablespoon (15 ml) of oil. Place the cherry in center. Arrange the lotus seeds, red dates and candied fruits in circles around the bottom and up to the edge of the bowl, glazed-side down.

Spread a layer of the rice mixture over the fruits carefully so as not to spoil the design. Spoon a layer of red bean paste over the rice. Cover it with another layer of rice. Pack it tightly.

Place the bowl on a rack in a pot or steamer. Cover. Steam it over boiling water 1 hour. Remove the pudding carefully by running a flexible spatula around the edge. Put a serving plate over the bowl and invert the bowl.

For the Sweet Almond Sauce

Boil the sugar in the water in a small saucepan, stirring until the sugar dissolves. Stir in the almond extract. Add the cornstarch slurry to the pan, and bring to a simmer to thicken. Drizzle the sauce over the pudding and serve.

THAI ICED COFFEE

Legend has it that what gives Thai coffee its distinctive nutty flavor is tamarind roasted together with the coffee. I'm not sure how true that is, but I love Thai coffee because it's strong without being too bitter. Some street vendors sub in evaporated or condensed milk for the half-and-half. I personally like using the half-and-half; it's a cleaner flavor. You can also use this recipe for an ice cream base.

SERVES 4

4 cups (960 ml) water

¼ cup (50 g) packaged Thai coffee mix

1 cup (200 g) sugar, or to taste

3 tbsp (45 ml) half-and-half

Bring the water to a boil in a medium saucepan. Stir in the Thai coffee mix. Simmer it over medium-low heat for about 20 minutes. Stir in the sugar, to taste. Strain the coffee through a sieve lined with cheesecloth. Chill it down in the fridge for a few hours; you can hold it up to two weeks in the fridge.

When ready to serve, fill a tall glass with ice. Pour the coffee over the ice, leaving about ½ inch (13 mm) of room at the top. Top with half-and-half and insert straw. Make sure the drinker uses that straw to mix the half-and-half thoroughly before drinking.

Pro Tip: Use a sieve lined with a clean tea towel to strain the coffee.

HOMEMADE INSTANT CHAI TEA MIX

This instant-mix recipe is for when you don't want to go through the ritual of brewing loose-leaf tea and steeping whole spices. You can place the mix in mason jars and wrap with twine for a great homemade foodie gift.

When you are craving a sweet spiced-tea treat, you just spoon the mix into your favorite mug, add hot water and you are set!

MAKES ABOUT 6 CUPS (750 G) OF MIX

1 cup (125 g) dry milk powder

1 cup (125 g) powdered nondairy creamer

2½ cups (545 g) sugar

1½ cups (190 g) unsweetened instant tea

2 tsp (10 g) ground ginger

2 tsp (10 g) ground cinnamon

1 tsp ground cloves

1 tsp ground cardamom

Place all the ingredients in a blender. Pulse a few times until totally combined—the mix should be one consistent color. Store it in an airtight container.

To serve, place 2 heaping tablespoons (30 g) of the Chai tea mixture in your favorite mug, and add 6 to 8 ounces (180–240 ml) of hot water. Stir well and enjoy.

THAI ICED TEA

Thai tea is very similar to Indian chai tea. The base is black tea with spices like vanilla, cloves and cardamom added in. It's supposed to be super sweet and served over a ton of ice, but by making it at home, you can control the amount of sweetness. You can find packaged Thai tea mix on the Internet with a few clicks. It's so much easier than making it on your own.

SERVES 4

4 cups (960 ml) water

½ cup (95 g) packaged Thai tea mix

1 cup (200 g) sugar

3–4 tbsp (45–60 ml) half-and-half

Bring the water to a boil in a medium saucepan. Stir in the Thai tea mix. Simmer it over medium-low heat for about 20 minutes. Stir in the sugar, to taste. Strain the tea through a sieve lined with cheesecloth. Chill it down in the fridge for a few hours. It will keep, refrigerated, for up to 2 weeks.

When ready to serve, fill a tall glass with ice. Pour the tea over the ice, leaving about ½ inch (13 mm) of room at the top. Top with half-and-half and insert straw. Make sure the drinker uses that straw to mix the half-and-half thoroughly before drinking.

*See photo.

> **Pro Tip:** Use a sieve lined with a clean tea towel to strain the coffee.

STOCKS, STAPLES AND BUILDING BLOCKS

These are the foundational recipes for almost any meal. In this chapter, you're going to learn how to make the many types of rice to eat with your perfect Asian meal and make those great fried-rice dishes. I get the question about rice cookers all the time. Do you need one? If you aren't making rice more than twice a week, I say no way. Invest your money in a heavy-lidded saucepan; it's perfect for making rice and way more useful. The secrets to making great rice are good-quality rice, water-to-rice ratios and heat control. All will be revealed in the pages ahead.

All the soup stocks are also here. It's OK to cheat a bit if you want to use store-bought broth. You can use boxed broth in any recipe that requires bones. But for Pete's sake, please fortify the broth with the various aromatics and seasonings called for in the recipes. This will be a nice compromise.

THAI CHICKEN STOCK

This recipe is the base stock for the two most well-known Thai soups in the world, Tom Yum (spicy and sour, here) and Tom Kha Gai (coconut chicken soup, here). I think making this from scratch versus using a store-bought stock makes all the difference. You'll taste more layers of flavors and deeper savoriness. This can also be a delicious stand-alone soup, but you'll need to add a little salt or fish sauce to finish it.

MAKES 2 QUARTS (1.9 L)

1 chicken carcass or whole chicken cut into 8 pieces

Cold water to cover

8 cups (1.9 L) water

3″ (8-cm) piece thinly sliced galangal

2 stalks lemongrass, thick lower portion only, pounded

2–3 kaffir lime leaves

2 cloves garlic, peeled

1 large shallot, peeled and sliced

2 Thai chilies, pounded with the knife

Place a cut-up whole chicken or boned carcass in an 8-quart (7.6-L) stockpot and cover with cold water. Bring the bones to a boil and simmer for 5 minutes. Remove the bones and rinse and wash under running cold water until the sediment and scum have washed away. Dump out the cooking liquid from the pot and give it a quick rinse. Return the chicken carcass to the pot and cover with 8 cups (1.9 L) of fresh water. Bring the stock to a full rolling boil over high heat, then reduce to a simmer.

Add the galangal, lemongrass, kaffir lime leaves, garlic cloves, shallots and chilies to the pot and allow to simmer. Skim off the foam and fat often, and continue to simmer for about 1½ hours. Skim off any additional fat and strain the stock through a cheesecloth-lined sieve. If not using this stock immediately, you can hold it for about a week in the fridge or freeze it for 6 months.

DASHI STOCK

Dashi is the foundation soup stock for all Japanese dishes. All the quintessential dishes from ramen, tempura sauce, miso soup and udon all require it. You can buy the instant version, called hon-dashi, but it's full of MSG. Making it from scratch is the way to go. It's simple in idea, being a fish stock. But unlike a western fish stock made from boiling bones and some mirepoix, it's a lot more like team-making. The key is katsuobushi, also known as bonito flakes. Bonito is a cousin to tuna. It's filleted, smoked, then dried until rock hard. This concentrates the umami and removes the fishiness. Then it's shaved super thin into sheets. These sheets, katsuobushi, are steeped with kombu. Kombu is sea kelp leaves. It's also dried into hard sheets. The drying process removes the water, and natural sea salt is concentrated and is pure umami. That white sea salt from kombu is what MSG chemically tries to mimic.

MAKES 3 TO 4 CUPS (711–946 ML)

4 cups (960 ml) cold water

1 (4" x 4" [10- x 10-cm]) piece giant kelp (kombu)

2 cups (24 g) dried bonito flakes (katsuobushi)

In a medium pot, combine the cold water with the giant kelp. Heat the pot on medium. As the water comes to a simmer, you'll see tiny bubbles start to form on the bottom of the pot. Turn off the heat and remove the kombu. If the kombu is allowed to boil, the stock will taste grassy and metallic.

Bring the temp up to medium; once the water starts to simmer, gently rain in the bonito flakes. Let the flakes steep without stirring, about 1 minute. Remove from the heat and strain through a cheesecloth-lined sieve.

CHINESE CHICKEN SOUP STOCK

My Cantonese grandmother made soup for every meal, as is the custom in southern China. I watched her make hundreds of soups over the years, and she always started with this very broth. This is the mother of all Chinese soup dishes. It's the broth for all wonton and noodle soups. It's also a stock for any and all dishes that require soup, like congee. You can also add your favorite vegetables to this, like bok choy and some scallions, to make the perfect hearty vegetable soup.

MAKES 1 GALLON (3.8 L)

1 whole chicken, cut into 8 pieces (skin off)

1 lb (450 g) pork neck bones

4 qt (3.8 L) cold water

2″ (5-cm) piece ginger

1 clove garlic, pounded

2 scallions, chopped into thirds

½ tsp white peppercorns

2 tbsp (30 ml) oyster sauce

Salt to taste

Bring 3 quarts (2.9 L) water to a boil in a large stockpot. Add the chicken pieces and pork neck bones, and boil for about 3 to 5 minutes. This will bring out blood and scum. Pour off the water and rinse the chicken.

Place the chicken and pork back into the pot. Add 4 quarts (3.8 L) of cold water and all the ingredients except salt. Bring the water to a boil and cover it. Reduce the heat to a medium simmer and leave the lid slightly cracked. Simmer it for about 2 to 4 hours, skimming the scum occasionally. Season with salt to taste.

Let the stock cool, then strain out and discard the solids. Stock can be refrigerated for up to 4 or 5 days.

INDIAN NAAN BREAD

This is my all-purpose naan, flat bread, pita and grilled pizza dough recipe! Perfect for serving with hummus or making your own grilled pizzas at home.

YIELDS 7 PIECES

1¼ cups (300 ml) warm water

1 tbsp (12 g) instant yeast

½ tbsp (8 g) sugar

1 extra-large egg

⅛ cup (30 ml) olive oil

¾ cups (165 ml) unsweetened plain yogurt

4½ cups (1.07 kg) unbleached bread flour, plus more for kneading

¼ cup (40 g) cornmeal

½ tsp baking powder

½ tbsp (7 g) salt

In the mixing bowl of a stand mixer, combine the warm water, instant yeast and sugar. Stir with a whisk until it's combined. Let it stand until a thick raft forms on top, about 10 to 15 minutes.

In a separate bowl, beat the egg, olive oil and yogurt until well combined. Add this to the water-yeast mixture.

Add the bread flour, corn meal, baking powder and salt to the mixture and knead on low speed with the dough hook attachment for 10 minutes. Stop the mixer and scrape down the sides of the bowl, releasing the dough from the sides. Continue mixing it on low speed, until the dough completely pulls away from the sides of the bowl, about 5 more minutes. The dough should be smooth, soft and slightly sticky.

Remove the bowl from the mixer and scrape down the sides of the bowl, releasing the dough. Cover it and let it stand in a warm spot until it doubles in volume, about 1 hour.

Turn out the dough on a very lightly floured work surface. Gently deflate the dough by punching it down. Scale it into 3- to 4-ounce (84- to 114-g) portions. Round the portions into balls and space them 2 inches (5 cm) apart on a sheetpan lightly dusted with flour. Cover it loosely with a towel or plastic wrap. Let it stand in a warm spot for about 15 to 20 minutes or until the balls are puffy and tender when poked with a finger.

Roll the balls into 8- to 9-inch (20- to 23-cm) rounds. Lightly dust them with flour to prevent the rounds from sticking to each other.

Preheat your grill to high and allow to preheat at least 10 minutes. This can also be cooked in a cast-iron skillet over a stove. Lightly spray raw bread rounds with oil and place them on the preheated grill. Once the rounds brown and puff, turn them over, about 45 seconds. Continue cooking them for an additional 45 seconds. Stack them on top of each other to prevent the rounds from drying out.

SUSHI RICE

Sushi was originally a method for preserving fish. The rice was heavily pickled and layers of fish and rice were pressed together to cure the fish. Later the practice of eating the fish raw with a less seasoned rice became fashionable. The word sushi literally translates to "vinegared rice," so you can understand how important it is. You can think about the rice as the starch and the seasoning for the raw fish. The additional benefit of the sushi rice is that the vinegar raises the pH, which helps make eating the raw fish even more safe.

MAKES ABOUT 6 CUPS (1.5 KG)

3 cups (700 g) sushi rice

3 cups (711 ml) water

6 oz (180 ml) unseasoned rice vinegar

5 tbsp (65 g) sugar

¼ cup (62 g) sea or kosher salt

4″ (10-cm) square piece kombu

Place the rice in a fine sieve and rinse under cold running water. Massage the rice as you rinse it until the water runs clear and drain well. Add the rice and water to a rice cooker and cook for 20 minutes. If using a pot, place the rice and water in a 2-quart (1.8-L) heavy saucepot with a tight-fitting lid. Cover and bring to a boil over high heat, reduce the heat to low and cook for 20 minutes. Remove from the heat and rest 20 minutes, until all the liquid is absorbed and the rice is shiny and tender.

In a separate small saucepan, combine rice vinegar, sugar, salt and kombu. Cook over low heat, stirring constantly until the sugar and salt are dissolved. This rice vinegar can be mixed and held for weeks before using.

Transfer the rested rice to a large wooden salad bowl and delicately spread into an even layer using a silicone spatula. Let it rest again for about 15 minutes undisturbed. Drizzle the vinegar mixture slowly all over the rice. Work the rice and vinegar together by gently folding, being careful not to smash any rice grains. You can press any large lumps apart and fold the rice back into the vinegar. Taste the rice and, if desired, add more of the vinegar mixture. Fold until any lumps are broken up and the rice is uniform and shiny. You can hold the sushi rice in a large lidded Dutch oven lined with plastic until you're ready to make sushi.

KOREAN RED BEAN MIXED RICE

Many have wondered how to make that delicious rice often eaten with Korean BBQ. Chewy short-grain rice tinted red with chewy red beans is fun to eat. It's kind of like the granola of rice, with its different textures. The secret is adzuki beans. They are tiny red beans that originated in China and migrated all over Asia. They are packed with protein and a staple to the macrobiotic diet—not that most of us really care. But for those who do, it's a great stealth health ingredient.

MAKES 4 CUPS (1 KG)

⅓ cup (80 g) adzuki beans, dry

2 cups plus 1¼ cup (480 ml plus 300 ml) water, divided

1 cup (250g) short-grain rice

Soak beans in about 2 cups (480 ml) of water for about 4 hours to overnight. Drain the beans with a fine mesh strainer but reserve 1 cup (240 ml) of the soaking water. Transfer the beans and rice to a 1-quart (946-ml) saucepan or rice cooker and add 1¼ cup (300 ml) of water, plus the reserved 1 cup (240 ml) of soaking water.

Bring your heat to high. As soon as the water reaches a boil, give everything a good stir, reduce to a low simmer and cover the pot. After 20 minutes, turn off the burner, remove the pot from the heat and let it sit for at least 15 minutes before fluffing with a fork and serving.

PERFECT JASMINE RICE

Jasmine rice is quickly becoming the world's most popular table rice. It's perfect because it has all the qualities that one looks for. It is long grain, fragrant and has great mouthfeel. Asians have been cooking jasmine rice for hundreds of years, and you can bet that a measuring cup has almost never been used. The funky thing about jasmine rice is, the more rice you cook, the less water you need. So it's all about the finger method—no not the one you're thinking of, the index finger.

MAKES 2 CUPS (500 G)

1 cup (230 g) long-grain jasmine rice
1¼ cups (300 ml) water

Add the rice to a fine mesh strainer and rinse under cold running water while swirling with your fingers to wash the rice. Wash the rice for about 30 seconds and then rinse for about a minute.

Add the rice to a 2-quart (1.8-L) saucepan. Insert your index until touching the top of the rice with your fingertip. Add water until the water just reaches the first crease of your finger. Bring your heat to high. As soon as the water reaches a boil, give everything a good stir, reduce to a low simmer and cover the pot. After 20 minutes, turn off the burner, remove the pot from the heat and let it sit for at least 15 minutes before fluffing with a fork and serving.

 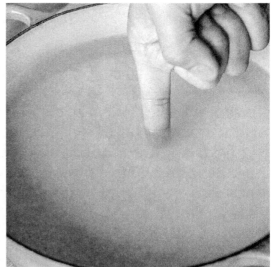

BROWN RICE

Brown rice is quickly becoming more popular than white, but it's a little trickier to cook. Brown rice still has the bran attached. This extra layer of armor takes a little more water and a little more time to break down. This recipe uses the finger method just like the White Jasmine Rice on the previous page—the classic way to get perfectly cooked rice every time. It will work on almost all common types of brown rice, including long grain, short grain and jasmine.

MAKES 2 CUPS (500 G)

1 cup (200 g) brown rice

1¾ cups (420 ml) water

Add the rice to a fine mesh strainer and rinse under cold running water while swirling with your fingers to wash the rice. Wash the rice for about 30 seconds and then rinse for about a minute.

Add the rice to a 2-quart (1.8-L) saucepan. Insert your index until touching the top of the rice with your fingertip. Add water until the water just reaches the first crease of your finger. Bring your heat to high. As soon as the water reaches a boil, give everything a good stir, reduce to a low simmer and cover the pot. After 30 minutes, turn off the burner, remove the pot from the heat and let it sit for at least 15 minutes before fluffing with a fork and serving.

THAI STICKY RICE

Most "sticky" rice is short grain, like the kind you eat in sushi. And fragrant rice is usually long grain, like jasmine or basmati. Thai sticky rice is uniquely fragrant, sticky and long grain. It's grown only in the region between Thailand and Vietnam. It's one of the few rice varieties that you actually steam. It soaks up much of its water during the soaking process. Although we call most rice steamed rice, it's almost all boiled. A Thai sticky rice steamer is the best tool for cooking sticky rice, and they are cheap to buy.

SERVES 4

2 cups (500 g) Thai sweet rice

4 cups (960 ml) water

Place 2 cups (500 g) of sticky rice in a medium bowl and cover with 4 cups (960 ml) of room-temperature water. Soak for at least 3 hours, preferably overnight.

A Thai bamboo sticky rice steamer consists of two pieces: an aluminum pot and a bamboo basket. When ready to cook, transfer the soaked rice into the bamboo basket. Give the basket a strong downward tap to seat the rice well against the bottom of the basket. Add 3 cups (710 ml) of fresh water into the pot. Bring the water to a boil over high heat.

Once the water in the pot comes to a boil, insert the basket into the pot and cover with a medium pot lid. Steam for 10 minutes, or until the rice starts to become sticky, then give the rice a flip. Flipping means you grip the basket by the sides and jerk up and slightly forward like you are flipping a pancake. Let the rice ball steam for another 10 minutes or until the rice is soft and yields to the touch. Be careful not to get burned by the steam as you're lifting the lid off the basket. Remove from heat; rest for 10 minutes covered and serve warm.

FRAGRANT COCONUT RICE

This is a recipe I make at our restaurants and is always a crowd favorite. It's perfect for the times you just want something a little richer and more decadent than plain rice. It's creamy and very aromatic. Add a few tablespoons of sugar or honey if you really want to feel guilty the next day.

MAKES 4 CUPS (1 KG)

2 tbsp (30 ml) vegetable oil

½ onion, finely chopped

2 cups (450 g) jasmine rice

2 tsp (10 g) kosher salt

1 cup (240 ml) canned coconut milk

2½ cups (590 ml) water

2 whole cloves

1 whole cinnamon stick

2 bay leaves

Heat the oil over high in a 2-quart (1.8-L) saucepan. Add the onion and stir-fry for 1 minute, until translucent. Add the rice and salt and sauté for 1 more minute.

Add the coconut milk and water and bring the mixture to a boil. Stir in the whole cloves, cinnamon and bay leaves. Adjust the heat to low until lightly simmering.

Cover and cook the rice undisturbed for 20 minutes or until all the liquid is completely absorbed. Turn off your heat and allow it to rest for at least 20 minutes to 1 hour, covered. Fluff, remove the spices and serve warm.

SAUCES AND DIPPERS

I've included these recipes in their own chapter because they are super useful on their own. You'll want quick access to them because they are the perfect accompaniments or finishing touches to your meals.

Be like a chef: If you find yourself making any of these often or crave them, make them in large batches! In the restaurant, I would multiply these by about 5 or 10 and keep them in airtight containers or in squeeze bottles. That way, they are at the ready when you need the perfect sauce. And please stop buying that premade garbage in bottles off the shelf. They are full of MSG and other junk you don't want to be consuming.

Enjoy making your sauce from scratch and playing with ingredients and flavors at home.

BOMB-ASS HOMEMADE SRIRACHA

If you love really spicy Sriracha, reverse the proportions of the serrano and jalapeño peppers. And if you think that's not gonna be hot enough for you, sub the chilies for scotch bonnets and Thai chilies. I'm not responsible for the burning of your mouth or bottom if you go this route! This is also a great way to preserve your once-a-year chilies like New Mexico Hatch or home grown.

MAKES ABOUT 2 CUPS (480 ML)

¾ lb (340 g) red jalapeños, stemmed and roughly chopped

¼ lb (115 g) red serranos, stemmed and roughly chopped

½ lb (230 g) green jalapeños, stemmed and roughly chopped

4 cloves garlic

⅛ cup (25 g) sugar

⅛ cup (25 g) brown sugar

1–2 tsp (5–10 g) salt

½ cup (120 ml) distilled white vinegar

1 tsp xanthan gum (optional, to help stabilize the sauce for long holding)

Place the peppers, garlic, sugars and salt in a food processor and pulse until roughly chopped. Transfer the mixture to a clean container, cover and let sit at room temperature. A mason jar with a loosely fitting lid or a clean bowl with plastic wrap will work.

Fermentation should begin in about 2 days. When bubbles begin to form, stir your "mash" once or twice a day to combine and help it settle. Continue until the mixture stops bubbling, about 6 to 8 days.

Transfer the mash to a blender, add the vinegar, and purée until very smooth. Strain the sauce through a fine sieve. Add the xanthan gum and purée again until smooth and thick. Store your sauce in squeeze bottles in the fridge for up to 3 months!

GRANDMA'S SECRET HOT SAUCE

This was the dipping sauce my grandmother would make for her pan-fried pot stickers. To this day, the flavors remind me of her cooking. It's one of those sauces that is so simple yet perfect. I've made it many times in my professional career, and it constantly amazes and bewilders all the chefs who have tried it. Now it's yours to pass on and impress with.

MAKES ABOUT ¾ CUP (180 ML)

¼ cup (60 ml) soy sauce

¼ cup (60 ml) Sriracha

¼ cup (50 g) sugar

Combine all the ingredients in a small bowl and whisk together until the sugar is dissolved.

HOISIN PEANUT DIPPING SAUCE

This is my favorite sauce for fresh spring rolls but can make a great dipper for satay, chicken wings or anything. The sweet hoisin flavor is very forward and pairs well with duck too.

MAKES ABOUT 1 CUP (240 ML)

½ cup (120 ml) hoisin sauce

3 tbsp (45 ml) creamy peanut butter

¼ cup (60 ml) water

1 tbsp (15 ml) rice vinegar

Prepare the sauce by combining all the ingredients until thoroughly mixed.

PEANUT SAUCE

This recipe was traditionally eaten with satay but has morphed into being a mother sauce. You can eat it as a dipper with finger foods like ribs and pot stickers. Folding it into cooked noodles makes an amazing Asian pasta. Thinning it out with more vinegar makes a great salad dressing. Use this recipe whenever you need a great peanut sauce. Chunky or smooth is totally up to you.

MAKES ABOUT 2½ CUPS (600 ML)

2 tbsp (30 ml) vegetable oil

1 tbsp (16 g) red curry paste, or more to taste

2 cups (490 ml) coconut milk

2 tbsp (30 g) chunky peanut butter, or more to taste

2 tbsp (30 ml) fish sauce

½ tsp rice vinegar

2 tbsp (30 g) sugar, or more to taste

Heat the oil in a small saucepan over high heat. When hot, stir-fry the curry paste for about a minute or until very fragrant and thick.

Stir in the coconut milk and bring it to a boil; cook for 2 minutes while constantly stirring. Be careful not to let it boil over. Add the peanut butter, stirring constantly, until the sauce begins to thicken and come together, about 2 to 3 minutes.

Reduce the heat to a simmer and add the fish sauce, rice vinegar and sugar. Cook the sauce for 1 minute more, then remove it from the heat. An oily film will rise to the top; skim it off if you wish.

VIETNAMESE NUOC CHAM DIPPING SAUCE

This is the orange sauce always served with Vietnamese dishes. From crispy spring rolls to rice plates to cold noodle dishes. A great hack is to add a bit of chili garlic sauce to finish. It adds an amazing kick.

MAKES ABOUT 1 CUP (240 ML)

2 tbsp (30 ml) lime juice

¼ cup (60 ml) fish sauce

¼ cup (60 ml) water

1 tbsp (15 ml) rice vinegar

¼ cup (50 g) sugar

1 garlic clove, minced

1 Thai chile, finely chopped

Combine all the ingredients and stir to dissolve the sugar completely.

KOREAN GOCHUJANG SAUCE

I love this for so many dishes. From chicken wings to adding to burgers and dogs, even dipping French fries in. This is also great for topping Korean rice and grain bowls. The sugar, vinegar and sesame oil temper the heat of the chili paste perfectly.

MAKES ABOUT 1 CUP (240 ML)

¼ cup (60 g) Korean fermented hot pepper paste (gochujang)

⅓ cup (67 g) sugar

⅓ cup (80 ml) soy sauce

1 tbsp (15 ml) sesame oil

Combine all the ingredients and stir to dissolve the sugar completely.

SRIRACHA MAYO AND WASABI MAYO

These are two food-truck staples—uber useful! Sriracha Mayo is great for making a quick spicy tuna. Both are great for Asian versions of burgers, dogs and any other street-food fare.

MAKES SCANT ¾ CUP (170 G) OF EACH

Sriracha Mayo

½ cup (113 g) mayonnaise

2 tbsp (30 ml) Sriracha chili sauce

1 tsp sesame oil

Wasabi Mayo

2 tbsp (10 g) wasabi powder (horseradish powder)

2 tbsp (30 ml) water

½ cup (113 g) mayonnaise

Stir each set of ingredients together until thoroughly mixed.

TEMPURA DIPPING SAUCE (TENTSUYU)

Although this is the classic tempura dipping sauce, I think it's a great stand-alone recipe as a cold or hot noodle broth.

MAKES 1¼ CUPS (300 ML)

½ cup (120 ml) Dashi Stock

3 oz (90 ml) mirin

3 oz (90 ml) light soy sauce

1 tsp finely grated ginger

Prepare the dipping sauce by combining the ingredients in a saucepan over medium-high heat, bringing just to a boil. Remove from the heat and use warm or store in the fridge until you're ready to use it.

TERIYAKI SAUCE

This is the sauce for the Salmon Teriyaki and it's a great sauce to keep in the fridge. You can use it as a marinade and a finishing sauce for any meat, seafood or vegetable.

MAKES ABOUT 1¼ CUPS (300 ML)

2 oz (60 ml) sake

3 oz (90 ml) mirin

4 oz (120 ml) soy sauce

3 tbsp (45 g) sugar

1 tbsp (8 g) cornstarch combined with 1 tbsp (15 ml) water

Mix all the ingredients in a small saucepan and bring to a simmer over medium heat; whisk until the sugar dissolves and the sauce bubbles and thickens slightly.